CHARLESTON STYLE

Then and Now

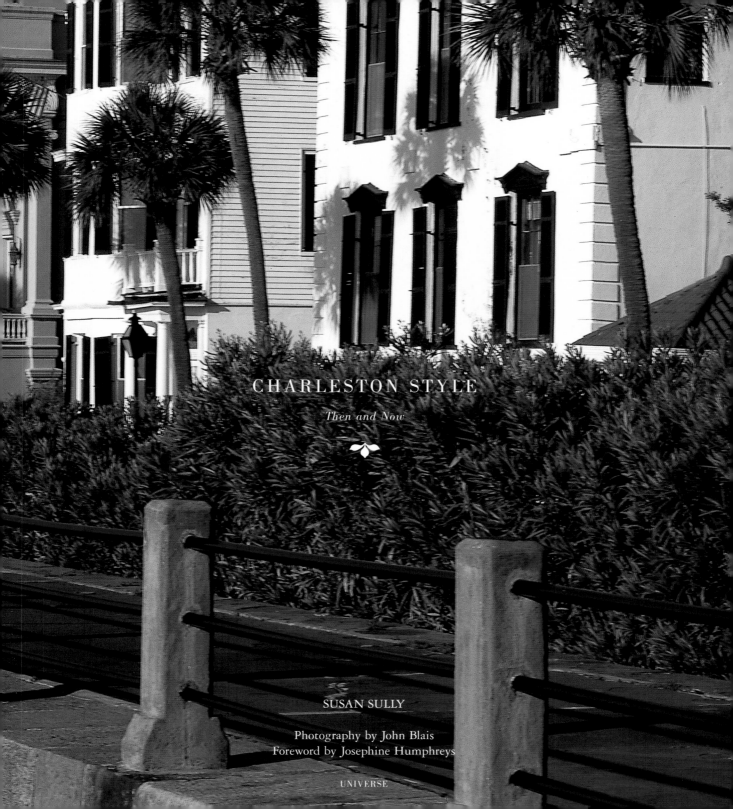

CHARLESTON STYLE

Then and Now

SUSAN SULLY

Photography by John Blais
Foreword by Josephine Humphreys

UNIVERSE

First published in the United States of
America in 2003 by Universe Publishing
A Division of Rizzoli International
Publications, Inc.
300 Park Avenue South
New York, NY 10010

Revised edition of *Charleston Style: Past
and Present,* first published in 1999 in
the United States of America by
Rizzoli International Publications, Inc.

2003 2004 2005 2006
/ 10 9 8 7 6 5 4 3 2 1
Printed in China
Designed by Opto Design
Library of Congress Control Number:
2002112180

ACKNOWLEDGMENTS

With this book, I offer my gratitude to
Charleston and its people, who together
cast a spell of beauty and graciousness over
anyone fortunate enough to come within
their power. In particular, I thank those
many people who welcomed me into their
houses, gardens, and lives while I researched
this book, both those whose homes are
featured as well as those whose are not, due
to space limitations, even though they
provided important inspiration. The staff
of Historic Charleston Foundation and
Historic Charleston Reproductions were most
especially helpful and generous with their
time and expertise, especially Cornelia Pelzer,
Renée Marshall, and Jonathan Poston,
whose extraordinarily comprehensive book
The Buildings of Charleston provided inva-
luable information. Special thanks are due
to Marty Whaley Adams,
Susan Virginia Hull, Robert P. Stockton,
author of *The Great Shock: The Effects of the
1886 Earthquake on the Built Environment
of Charleston, South Carolina*, and Mary Pope
Waring for their guidance and friendship.
I would like to thank my editors David
Morton and Alex Tart for their assistance and
enthusiasm, and Josephine Humphreys for
gracing this book with such a beautiful
foreword. I wish to thank Professor Vincent
Scully of Yale University for teaching me
to look at the decorative arts with an eye
attuned to beauty, mystery, and humor.
And finally, I wish to thank my husband,
parents, sister, and friends, without
whose encouragement I would not have
been able to complete this daunting and
delightful project.

CONTENTS

TO MY FAMILY AND FRIENDS,
ESPECIALLY MY HUSBAND, THOMAS SULLY,
AND TO THE PEOPLE OF CHARLESTON

Beautiful as a dream, tinged with romance, consecrated by
tradition, glorified by history, rising from the very bosom of the waves,
like a fairy city created by the enchanter's wand. . . .

-ARTHUR MAZYCK, *GUIDE TO CHARLESTON, ILLUSTRATED* (PUBLISHED 1875)

All changed, changed utterly; A terrible beauty is born.

—WILLIAM BUTLER YEATS, *EASTER, 1916*

FOREWORD

By Josephine Humphreys

As a child I spent many long spring afternoons looking down upon the corner of Church and Water streets from the window seat of my garret room, in a trance of intensely agitated comfort. The corner was always sunny, and I could see the harbor glistening at the foot of Water Street. To the south, Church Street bent into shadow, under the cover of oaks. Sometimes the Shrimp Man came singing or the Broom Man came tapping his cane, and there was something in the air. It may have been sea mist or pollen, or heat, dazzle, irony, memory, sin, longing—I don't know. But I couldn't tear myself away, I was under the spell.

That was a good house, my grandmother's via a divorce settlement, and I loved it madly. The living room was bright and airy with an ornate ceiling medallion of flowers and wreathing leaves, and the dining room had French doors opening onto the piazza. But the reason for my love had less to do with the actual house than with where it was and what it let in: Charleston itself. I felt the town was all mine— its secrets, its constantly surprising beauty, faults both comic and tragic, depths of vanity and stamina, ruthless pride and startling good-heartedness.

As it turns out I never did tear myself away— not permanently. I've counted myself a Charlestonian for more than half a century now, and although the place has remodeled itself several times over, its essential air is the same. What does change is how we breathe it in—whether automatically as a matter of routine, or joyfully, in celebration. These days Charleston houses seem more joyful than they used to, although when I recall the past I may be recalling myself more than anything else, my own eras.

But I do think there was a time when you could enter any one of a hundred houses in the historic area and not be quite sure whether you had left home or not. Downtown Charleston living rooms were eerily similar from one house to the next, and the dining rooms (in my memory) virtually identical. I began to see a scary rigor in those formal rooms. They were relics, seldom used except during those daunting Charleston parties when the long mahogany dining table had been waxed to a sheen (my aunt used to climb up in her stocking feet and run an upright floor polisher back and forth the length of the table), and the food was laid out in the expected pattern: whole turkey at one end, ham at the other, pickled shrimp and green pepper jelly on the sides. At the time I was dismayed at the success of the whole Charleston effort, the incredible consistency of style and material and detail—but maybe it was no effort at all, only a natural mirror of a synchronized community.

In those days when a young person left home, no one grieved. It was understood that the runaways would come back. Eloping brides, liberal activists, ambitious entrepreneurs—all those who were sure they could not live Charleston lives—went off and then came home again, not in defeat or resignation

PAGES 6–7: THIS TINY BEDROOM IN THE HOME OF RANDOLPH MARTZ AND GENE WADDELL PROVIDES JUST SPACE ENOUGH FOR BED, BUST (OF ATHENA), AND FAN. PAGE 8: THE UNUSUAL STREET NUMBER OF THE JAMES MITCHELL HOUSE, 43 ½, REFERS TO THE MODERNIZED DEPENDENCY LOCATED BEHIND THE TRADITIONAL SHINGLE HOUSE, CONSTRUCTED CIRCA 1798. THE WROUGHT IRON GATE WAS DESIGNED BY A PREVIOUS RESIDENT IN THE 1930s.

but with a growing knowledge of what it means to be a native son or daughter of a place like this. It requires seeing into history, learning a complicated kind of loyalty not unlike that of marriage, and eventually understanding that you're home for good, to live the kind of Charleston life that's also your own; to do your work in your own place. The experience, I found out, is more exhilarating than world travel.

Nowadays the rooms of our houses still look to the past, but they draw from a wider range of tradition. And they do it with less austerity, more liberty and humor and inventiveness—qualities that were here all along but were kept under wraps. I tend to love best the more modest houses and the smaller rooms, those on the human rather than the grand scale; I'm afraid there's a danger the modest house will be crowded out someday. But I also believe that Charlestonians know how disastrous that outcome would be, and will guard against it. The city has always accommodated grandeur and modesty side by

side. Although we have never been without our pretensions, we've never quite trusted them either, and there remains a premium on the tiny garden, the cottage and carriage house, the narrow street.

And I think we have also learned to leave room for mystery, as Susan Sully's *Charleston Style: Then and Now* so eloquently reveals. With an eye for the distinctive style (or more important, an eye for the meaning of style), Sully demonstrates how the fashion of our rooms signifies the spirit of our time and place. She's showing the Charleston of a new golden age, more vigorous than ever before, still firmly rooted in history, drawing on it, and flourishing—yet at the same time somewhat dreamy and witty, like a bold girl at ease with herself, who knows how to laugh.

MANY FURNISHINGS IN THE WILLIAM PINCKNEY SHINGLER HOUSE DINING ROOM COME FROM DR. WILSON'S BOYHOOD HOME ON NEARBY WADMALAW ISLAND, WHERE PLANTERS GREW SEA ISLAND COTTON. THE EARLY-NINETEENTH-CENTURY SILVER EPERGNE IS USED ON HOLIDAYS AND SPECIAL OCCASIONS.

INTRODUCTION

The Remembrance of Things
Past and Present

Time refuses to stand still in Charleston, South Carolina. It swirls around in a vortex that leaves visitors and inhabitants alike breathlessly disoriented. The city demands an intense awareness of the present, with its rich textures, shifting light, heady scents, and clamorous urban sounds. And yet, the sight of an uninterrupted lane of nineteenth-century houses, the gesture of an antique steeple against the twilight sky, and the ancient sound of bells ringing changes all hark back to older times. The past infuses the present like the pungent tea leaves that once were cultivated on outlying plantations.

There are those who would rather stay the course of time, capturing the city in well-meaning nostalgia for the glory days "Before the War." Not unlike the remarkably fruitful Pax Romana, Charleston enjoyed nearly two hundred years of mounting prosperity and, with the exception of the Revolutionary War, almost uninterrupted peace until the Civil War destroyed its economic and social underpinnings. During those centuries, generations of Charlestonians constructed homes and civic structures that still remain to demonstrate the visions of their creators, the skill of their designers, and the labor of their builders. Pilgrims of history flock to these sites today, seeking absolution from the intervening century of progress-driven change.

Tragically, the city never regained its antebel-lum prosperity as changing labor systems and cultivation technology—not to mention the onslaught of the boll weevil—undermined first rice, then Sea Island cotton as critical staples of its agrarian economy. Although the discovery of phosphates beneath the rich soil of plantation fields fueled partial economic recovery, the new fortunes could not rival those of the eighteenth century, which gave Charleston the largest per capita wealth of any colonial American center. During this postwar era, Charlestonians gathered together their dignity and salvaged resources to re-create their town, not as a bright capital of the new South, but rather as a tribute to the old. Inhabitants restored what buildings they could and built new ones in the Victorian style with nods to vernacular form in the gaps left by war, storm, and the great earthquake of 1886.

When economic progress gathered momentum during the first few decades of the twentieth century, it brought along with it a host of threats to the city's architecture. With the popular advent of the motor car, street corners boasting great mansions were sited for demolition to make room for the construction of gasoline filling stations. As more and more tourists poured into town following World War I, architectural scavengers picked over the city, taking home pieces of buildings or whole structures like seashells or souvenirs. "The town found it had to protect itself from collectors of everything from ironwork to complete houses," wrote Samuel Gaillard Stoney in *This is Charleston* in 1944.[1] "Some of these last were taken

THE SIMPLE GEORGIAN DOOR SURROUND, DATING FROM THE 1772 CONSTRUCTION OF THE
WILLIAM GIBBES HOUSE, IS SURMOUNTED BY A DELICATELY DETAILED ADAMESQUE FRIEZE ADDED APPROXIMATELY TWENTY-FIVE
YEARS LATER. THE FANCIFUL ZUBER WALLPAPER IS AN EARLY-TWENTIETH-CENTURY EMBELLISHMENT.

down and carried off completely, from the brickwork of the basement to the timber of the roof."

When two venerable homes, the Joseph Manigault House and the Heyward-Washington House, were threatened by demolition and collectors, respectively, the city's people banded together to form the Society for the Preservation of Old Dwellings. Both of these houses are now museums that offer insight into the style and manners of old Charlestonians. Countless other historic structures owe their survival to this organization, now known as the Preservation Society of Charleston.

When important and beautiful structures continued to fall to the wrecking ball, the city passed pioneering legislation in 1931, designating America's first official historic district and creating a Board of Architectural Review to safeguard the city's architectural integrity. By 1947, Historic Charleston Foundation was created to provide the funds needed to preserve and protect the buildings that had been saved from destruction or wholesale exportation. Even more stringent regulation in the second half of this century was required to hinder the demolition of historic structures that continued through the 1970s.

As a result, Charleston today boasts a greater number of historic structures than any other city in America, and popular attention has moved away from preservation to the interpretation and restoration of old buildings. As block after block of faded structures receive long overdue facelifts, there are those Charlestonians who fear a "Disney-fication" of their town.

With structures that once proudly bore the telltale signs of age and tragedy now assuming youthful airs, some Charlestonians worry that the buildings will no longer testify as eloquently to the city's multi-layered past as they once did. The tincture of tragedy mingled with pride is a vital ingredient of the city's complex flavor, and one that is in danger of being overpowered by the cloying taste of nostalgia.

Certainly, there are plenty of neighborhoods off the tourists' beaten track whose gray, weathered structures still bear witness to the city's troubled past. Victorian jigsaw trim, once white, now hangs darkly from damp eaves, and tilting columns bear down heavily upon rotting wooden piazzas. While the inhabitants of these ramshackle tenements truly hunger for fresh paint and sound new carpentry, well-to-do homeowners south of Broad (the artery that forms the northern boundary of the city's most exclusive residential neighborhood) thirst for a hint of the lost decay that once lent peculiar charm to their now pristine enclave. Not more than three decades ago, grand homes and tumbledown tenements stood cheek by jowl below Broad Street. The stately tones of St. Michael's bells mingled with the syncopated rhythms of back-alley jugbands. A rich and spicy gumbo, laden with regional flavor, scented the city's humid air.

While there are always those who will mourn what is lost or faded away, there is much cause to celebrate in Charleston because so much has been saved. Visiting English actress Fanny Kemble's description

of Charleston in 1838 still aptly describes the city more than 150 years after she wrote these words: "The appearance of the city is highly picturesque, a word which can apply to none of the American towns . . . every house seems built to the owner's particular taste; and in one street you seem to be in an old English town, and in another in some continental city of France or Italy. This variety is extremely pleasing to the eye."[2]

What this description makes clear is that the people of Charleston, by weaving together a unique set of influences both foreign and domestic to suit their own lavish tastes, forged a distinctive regional style that transcends both time and trend. Perhaps the best spokesperson for this vernacular style is the Charleston single house—a ubiquitous form found nowhere else in such profusion and variety. While the earliest settlers in Charleston brought with them traditional English forms of architecture (Jacobean houses with curvilinear gables and massive Georgian double houses with high-raised basements and Palladian detail), by 1740 the single house emerged as the prevailing form.

"The single house was a creative response to the increasing scarcity of space in the city and was designed to mitigate the unpleasantness of hot, humid summers," explains Kenneth Severens in *Charleston, Antebellum Architecture and Civic Destiny.*[3] "With its narrow side directly on the street, the rectangular house with two rooms in each story grew tall to raise the main entertaining room to the level of the prevailing breeze which passed through a side piazza." Charlestonian John Drayton described the piazza's purpose in 1802, "as well for the convenience of walking thereon during the day as for preventing the sun's too great influence on the interior part of the house."[4] What these practical descriptions fail to convey is the delightful aspect of a row of antique single houses turning their bright white piazzas to face the breeze. While the basic form has

A ROOFLESS PORTICO OF CORINTHIAN COLUMNS IS ALL THAT REMAINS
OF THE BEAUX-ARTS–STYLE CHARLESTON MUSEUM BUILDING, WHICH BURNED IN 1980.

remained the same up to this day, as single houses continue to be built, embellishment has varied according to fashion. Single houses can be found adorned with Georgian, Adamesque, Greek Revival, Italianate, Second Empire, and Queen Anne elements. Ornate cornices, acanthus leaf capitals, paired brackets, mansard roofs, and ball-and-spindle work are frequent architectural motifs that have been grafted onto the Charleston single house over the centuries. While Charleston's domestic and civic architecture branched out to reflect a full range of European and American building types and styles, the enduring popularity of this vernacular form helps illustrate how the city's particular climate and culture called forth unique interpretations of borrowed styles. The very streetscape of the city illustrates the wayward personality of the place and its inhabitants. The Baroque city plan, devised in England and carried out by seventeenth-century surveyors, superimposed a rigid grid upon the watery, irregular peninsula. This plan, incorporating modern-day East Bay, Church, Meeting, and King streets, divvied up the land into massive city blocks six hundred feet per side. The Lords Proprietors sent over word instructing surveyors to "take care to lay streets broad and in straight lines."

Within less than fifteen years, however, settlers began to open narrow streets that broke the grid up into more convenient passageways. As the city grew, it spread beyond the proscribed walls. Creeks were filled and new roads cut that crisscrossed the grid with weaving diagonal threads. Before the eighteenth century ended, the city had already acquired the picturesque irregularity that today confounds tourists with a maze of narrow, one-way streets and dead-end alleys.

Clearly, Charlestonians were not content to fit within the mold. A list of the "firsts" forged by its inhabitants reveals their sybaritic tastes and appetites, entrepreneurial and bellicose impulses, and creative zeal. In 1700, the city formed the first public library in America and, in 1735, hosted the first opera performed in the British colonies. In 1744, Eliza Lucas Pinckney produced the first successful indigo crop, soon to become a staple of the economy. British North America's first musical organization, the St. Cecilia Society, was formed in 1762, followed by the first museum and chamber of commerce in 1773, first golf club in 1787, first successful sinking of a ship during warfare by a submarine in 1864, when the Hunley sank the Housatonic, and the nation's first official historic district, designated in 1931.[5] Taken alone, these innovations reveal the impulses of Charlestonians both to import and to adapt European modes and interweave them and protect them with the fruits of their own ingenuity. To list the tragedies, both man-made and natural, that have visited this city demonstrates the courage and unbending will that supported its residents' vision of a brave and beautiful new world.

Charleston was beset by calamity from the very beginning. In 1698, the city suffered from an earth-

quake, a smallpox epidemic that was the first of many, and a major fire that destroyed one quarter of the city. The following year, a yellow fever epidemic caused nearly two hundred deaths and a major hurricane swept over the town. Fires were frequent during the colonial era, and in 1740 the worst yet burned nearly half the city. Destructive hurricanes and cyclones smashed into the peninsula time and time again, in 1752, 1885, 1893, 1911, and most recently, in 1989, with Hurricane Hugo. One of the city's most devastating natural disasters occurred in 1886, when a massive earthquake shook the city with apocalyptic force, damaging many properties and taking ninety-two lives.[6]

"There was no intermission in the vibration of the mighty subterranean engine," wrote one survivor of the great quake. "From the first to the last it was a continuous jar, adding force with every moment, and, as it approached and reached the climax of its manifestation, it seemed for a few terrible seconds that no work of human hands could possibly survive the shocks. . . . The air was everywhere filled to the height of the houses with a whitish cloud of dry, stifling dust, arising from the lime and mortar of the shattered masonry, which, falling upon the pavement and stone roadway, had been reduced to powder."[7]

This natural calamity occurred less than twenty years after the man-made destruction of the federal bombardment of Charleston, which lasted nearly eighteen months—from 1863 to 1865. Although not the first bombardment and military occupation of Charleston (English troops vanquished the rebellious city in 1780 and occupied it for two years), it was the most destructive. Wartime Charlestonian Mrs. St. Julien Ravenel describes the appearance of the broken cityscape upon the conclusion of the Civil War.

"Everything was overgrown with rank, untrimmed vegetation," she wrote. "Not grass merely, but bushes, grew in the streets. The gardens looked as if the Sleeping Beauty might be within. The

THIS FOUR-POSTER BED WITH CANOPY FRAME FROM THE THOMAS HAMLIN HOUSE WAS MADE CIRCA 1830, MOST LIKELY BY A SOUTHERN ARTISAN. THE WHIMSICAL BEDSPREAD AND PILLOW SHAMS ARE CONTEMPORARY.

houses were indescribable: the gable was out of one, the chimneys fallen from the next; here a roof was shattered, there a piazza half gone; not a window remained. The streets looked as if filled with diamonds, the glass lay shivered so thick on the ground."[8]

When northern poet Amy Lowell came to view the ruined city fifteen years after the war, she wrote a poem entitled "Charleston, South Carolina" in which she proclaimed, "There is no dawn here, only sunset, / And an evening rain scented with flowers."[9] And yet, the sun continued to rise each day over the sparkling harbor, as Charlestonians put the war behind them, one more cataclysm to add to the city's chronicles.

Like the lost city of Atlantis or the found one of Pompeii, Charleston acquired a charismatic air of mystery. Tourists and historians flock to the place, compelled by its promise to transport them back in time. Yet the challenge facing Charleston's inhabitants now is not how to inhabit the past but rather how to live fully and creatively in the present in a place so laden with history. Just as Charlestonians in centuries past forged creative, individual adaptations of popular European and American decorative styles, so Charlestonians today interpret their own past both reverently and playfully to create a distinctive regional style. While visitors may come to Charleston expecting only to see into the past, they may be surprised to encounter fresh design as well.

As many Americans and Europeans seek alternatives to the coolly functional minimalism of modern architecture and the generic signs and borrowed symbols of postmodernism, they may find inspiration in Charleston's rooms—where the genuine and the generic, the familiar and the eccentric, the historical and the heretical sit side by side. Although the exterior of the city's buildings are, for the most part, restrained by stringent regulation from participating in this free-spirited bricolage, the interiors and gardens reveal another side of Charleston. Behind the city's demure facades lies a veritable Pandora's box of unruly impulses.

Within the proper walls of the Aiken-Rhett House, history indeed stands still in an eccentric reliquary, where dangling shreds of wallpaper and a broken harp display themselves to fervent eyes like bones of long-dead saints. On the far side of a venerable single house on Meeting Street, a thoroughly modern glass box encloses the facade of a brick outbuilding, louvered shutters, rusted iron hardware, and all. Behind another house's walls of Flemish bond, bright rooms adorned with Sumatran textiles, Burmese Buddhas, and Chinese chests transmute the familiar impulse of chinoiserie to an exotic extreme.

Within these rooms, one finds contemporary manifestations of the age-old tensions that define the city's charm: a love of both light and southern Gothic gloom, a simultaneous longing for and impatience with the past, a hunger for Western form and Eastern mystery. Gone, but not forgotten, the insistent past shines through these present-day places to create poignant reminders that reveal the city's soul.

Like the crumbling texture of a madeleine in Proust's great work, the time-worn walls and columns of Charleston unleash a torrent of memory, both sweet and bitter, at once personal and sociological, and always infinitely human. Beneath the heat of a semitropic sun, the very mortar of Charleston's buildings release collective memories that collide with the frankly sensual awareness demanded by the city's beauty. Yearning for the past mingles with mindfulness of the moment to spark not predictable nostalgia, but the far more capricious remembrance of things present.

A didactic treatment of the city's style, imprisoning it within the rigid chronology of unfolding architectural trends, would do Charleston disservice. There are as many ways of dealing with the past here as there are recipes for shrimp and hominy, the local delicacy that confounds expectations of diners from afar. For this reason, the houses and gardens visited in this book are grouped thematically to reveal their timeless influences. Chiaroscuro reveals and revels in the bright light and dark shadows that play over this southern town. Pentimento explores the city's dual tastes for tradition and innovation. Tradewinds evokes the salty air of a port city where imports from the West mingle with exotic flavors from the East. And Alchemy delves into the magic arts of fantasy and transformation that still shape Charleston's destiny.

1. Samuel Gaillard Stoney, *This is Charleston: A Survey of the Architectural Heritage of a Unique American City* (Charleston: The Carolina Art Association, 1944), 51.
2. quoted in Jonathan H. Poston for Historic Charleston Foundation, *The Buildings of Charleston: A Guide to the City's Architecture* (Columbia: University of South Carolina Press, 1997), 23.
3. Kenneth Severens, *Charleston, Antebellum Architecture and Civic Destiny* (Knoxville: The University of Tennessee Press, 1988), 7.
4. quoted in J. Thomas Savage, *The Charleston Interior* (Greensboro: Legacy Publications, 1995), 6.
5. Poston, *The Buildings of Charleston*, 16–22.
6. Ibid.
7. News & Courier, September 3, 1886; quoted in Robert P. Stockton, *The Great Shock* (Easley, S.C.: Southern Historical Press, 1986), 20–21.
8. quoted in Poston, *The Buildings of Charleston*, 51.
9. Amy Lowell, "Charleston, South Carolina," *The Complete Poetical Works of Amy Lowell* (Boston: Houghton Mifflin Company, 1995), 450.

BUILT BY A COTTON BROKER JUST YEARS BEFORE THE OUTBREAK OF THE CIVIL WAR, THIS GRAND EAST BATTERY MANSION FACES THE CHARLESTON HARBOR, WHICH WAS HEAVILY BOMBARDED BY FEDERAL FORCES. THE PORTICO AND SEMICIRCULAR PIAZZA WERE ADDED TWO DECADES AFTER THE WAR.

CHIAROSCURO

Light and Shadow

CHIAROSCURO

Light and Shadow

Chiaroscuro is an Italian word that means the play of light and shadow. Although the etymology is foreign, the translation is more than apt to describe the particular ambience of this seaside city. Perched on a peninsula bordered by the Ashley and Cooper Rivers, which some say join here to create the Atlantic Ocean, Charleston is prone to dramatic weather. Dark storms sweep over the city's walls with alarming regularity. Massive hurricanes of the ilk of Hurricane Hugo have been known to strike more than once, leaving the city in literal darkness for weeks at a time. Bright fires torched whole neighborhoods throughout the seventeenth, eighteenth, and nineteenth centuries. Blazing blooms of shell fire have illuminated the skies above the city's rooftops in several wars.

While these dramatic events contribute much to the poignance of this place, one that has survived miraculously intact despite threats of devastating scale, the light and shadow that play over the city's walls and gardens are usually of a less destructive kind. The semitropical sun bears down upon the peninsula with an intensity that demanded the articulation of specific architectural responses before the days of air conditioning. Linked in climate and colonial economy with the island of Barbados, Charleston spawned a type of architecture close in style to that of the island. The single house, with its deep piazza, provides the ideal form to capture cooling seaborn breezes and shade interior space. Deep masonry walls provide a sanctuary from the heat, and shuttered windows offer inhabitants the opportunity to baffle the sun's rays.

While the typical early American colonial house, with small rooms and low ceilings nestling around an open fire, suits northern climes, in Charleston, the large room with high ceilings and tall windows opening onto porches provides the southern solution. Indoor/outdoor living was a common mode in this place where fancy balls often spilled out onto piazzas and into gardens. Shuttered sleeping porches made the most of night's cool relief. Walled gardens shaded with the generous trees that grow here—giant live oaks draped with Spanish moss, dark-leaved magnolia grandiflora, and once upon a time, great elms—offer outdoor sanctuary from the sun. Punctuated by open lawns and beds that blossom brightly with foreign blooms—azaleas, camellias, gardenias, roses, and more—these gardens offer dappled compositions of light and dark and bright and somber palettes.

Throughout the day and into evening, the streets and rooftops participate in a dramatic shadow play. The air, dense with moisture, refracts the fickle light. At dawn and dusk, shades of orange, yellow, and pink drench the horizons. At night, the sky is often thick with purple hue. When storms are blowing in or out, shafts of impossibly yellow light rake over red-tiled roofs and dove-brown masonry.

LIKE MOST TRADITIONAL SINGLE HOUSES, THIS GEORGIAN HOME IS ENTERED BY AN
EXTERNAL DOOR THAT OPENS ONTO THE PIAZZA. FROM THE PIAZZA, A DOOR IN THE
MIDDLE OF THE LONG SIDE OF THE HOUSE OPENS INTO A CENTRAL STAIR HALL.

Shadows are dense and contours sharp throughout the hours on sunny days.

Within the city's rooms, the light and shadow are intensified. Permanent gloom enshrouds some homes whose shutters are perpetually fastened by the dense growth of coral vines and climbing roses. Wooden louvers admit no more than crooked bars of light. In other homes, the sun pours in through wavering panes of antique glass, outlining architectural details and enlivening the textures of polished wood and flowers arranged in gleaming vessels of glass and silver. Silver-backed mirrors turn back the sun and magnify it, filling the rooms with golden light.

As the sun's angle shifts with each season, it reminds Charleston's people not only of the passage of time, but also of its cyclic nature. Bright hours have blessed this city, where vast fortunes could be gathered up in a single season. Dark times have swept the town with natural and man-made disasters more often than most of its inhabitants would like to

count. Charleston has risen and fallen like the sun, and the play of light and shadow on its stones and trees and columns offer testimony to the city's staunch resilience.

A COPY OF JEAN-ANTOINE HOUDON'S BUST OF THOMAS JEFFERSON SEEMS AT HOME IN THIS GARRET OFFICE, WHERE GENE WADDELL WRITES VOLUMES ABOUT NEOCLASSICAL ARCHITECTURE. CHARLESTON SCULPTOR JOHN MICHEL'S BUST OF MARTZ KEEPS JEFFERSON AND WADDELL COMPANY.

CHARLESTON'S GARDENS BECKON TO PASSERS-BY FROM WITHIN WALLS
OF ANTIQUE BRICK AND ELABORATELY SCROLLED WROUGHT-IRON GATES.

CHARLESTON RELIQUARY

The Aiken-Rhett House
Historic Charleston Foundation

In 1839, after attending a party at the Aiken-Rhett House, Francis Kinloch Middleton wrote, "Last night I was at the handsomest ball I have ever seen. Two floors were entirely thrown open—the orchestra from the theatre played for the dancers—and the supper table was covered with a rich service of silver—lights in profusion, & a crowded handsomely dressed assembly."[1] In her journal, southern diarist Mary Boykin Chesnut describes a "perfect old Carolina style of living" that apparently delighted Jefferson Davis during a visit to the house in 1863, as well as Chesnut herself, who commented, "one does miss that sort of thing when away from home."[2]

The backdrop for these extravagant gatherings was one of Charleston's grandest urban mansions. Originally designed in 1817 as a Federal-style center hall dwelling, the building was located at the head of a public mall in the fashionable neighborhood of Wraggsborough, just slightly north and east of the unhealthily crowded lower peninsula. Built by a merchant who soon afterward experienced a reversal of fortune, the house passed into the hands of the Aiken family, who owned it for three generations, from 1827 until 1975.

During the occupancy of the house's most notable inhabitants, Governor William Aiken, Jr., and his wife, Harriet, the mansion at 48 Elizabeth Street underwent two ambitious remodelings. The first was a Greek Revival restyling in 1833, followed by an exuberant Rococo Revival expansion in 1858. These renovations involved repositioning the front door from the long facade to the sidewall, constructing a pair of arched marble staircases in the new entrance hall, and adding a ballroom, dining room, and art gallery, as well as window and door surrounds, chandeliers, plasterwork, and wall coverings that reflect the tastes of the times.

However, the most dramatic transformation in the appearance of the Aiken-Rhett House was wrought not by the hands of men, but by the passage of time and the sweeping economic and social change that was to relegate memories of lavish antebellum southern living to nostalgia. Following Governor Aiken's death in 1887, his wife closed off several rooms of the house with many furnishings intact and transformed the ballroom into a grand master bedroom. After her death, this room was shut up for seventy-nine years. Although the Aikens' daughter, Henrietta Aiken Rhett, and her children continued to use the house for another seventy-five years, little change was made except for the electrification of a few rooms and the sealing off of several others. Within and without, dilapidation set in.

By the time Governor Aiken's granddaughter-in-law turned the house over to the care of the Charleston Museum, it had been abandoned to vandals and the elements. When a curator from the museum entered it in 1975, opening many rooms for the first time in decades, the experience was not unlike the breaching of King Tutankhamen's tomb. "The box of keys was

THE ART GALLERY OF THE AIKEN-RHETT HOUSE, ADDED IN 1858, PROVIDES AN OPULENT ROCOCO SETTING WITH ORNATE PLASTER WORK AND CURVILINEAR NICHES IN WHICH EUROPEAN ARTWORK, COLLECTED BY GOVERNOR AND MRS. AIKEN, IS DISPLAYED.

formidable, every size, every shape, every material," wrote J. Kenneth Jones in his 1975 curator's report.[3]

"As the key turned in the weathered front door it was like entering another era," Jones continued. "The door creaked open, revealing the graceful marble double staircase with its dusty iron balustrade. Bits of broken glass from the shattered fanlight were scattered on the steps. . . . Everywhere there was peeling paint, tattered wallpaper and dust. . . . The French Empire Ormolu chandeliers, coated in black dust, were hanging with broken chains of prisms. Fallen pendants littered the floor." The only inhabitants remaining in the house were pigeons "nesting on sills between sash and shutters and sometimes in the rooms themselves. . . . They had been here so long they had inbred and were sparsely feathered. Many had deformed beaks. They all looked diseased."

Although the Aiken-Rhett House has been cleaned, stabilized, and preserved under the curatorship first of the Charleston Museum and now Historic Charleston Foundation, it retains a hushed, mysterious air. In the vast, echoing double parlor, the life-size portrait of Harriet Aiken still guards her now vacant domain. In the ballroom above, crooked bands of light penetrate the broken louvers of old shutters to gild the tattered edges of silk upholstery and shreds of loosened wallpaper. Beyond lies a ghostly chamber where a nineteenth-century foot bath and muslin-enshrouded dressing table seem to await the return of southern ladies and their servants. Even deeper into the private quarters of the house lies the master bedroom, furnished with a massive mahogany sleigh bed. The faded portrait of a child gazes plaintively from above the marble mantle that dominates one wall.

Today the Aiken-Rhett House remains not only as a testament to the changing lifestyles, tastes, and fortunes of its owners, but also of the servants who inhabited this compound. Behind the house lies one of the most intact nineteenth-century work yards not just in Charleston, but in America. Facing each other across a brick-paved courtyard are a pair of two-story buildings, a carriage house on one side and kitchen and slaves' quarters on the other. Below this area stretches a lawn planted with an avenue of magnolia trees, enclosed by a high brick wall that ends with a large gate and a pair of privies.

All four of the outbuildings are decorated with Gothic details; even the horse stalls are outlined with pointed arches. While the Gothic Revival style achieved little popularity among primary houses in Charleston, it was frequently employed in the design of outbuildings. Some architectural historians hypothesize that this signaled the gentry's nostalgia for feudal England, and that some drew parallels between feudalism and their own labor system, comparing slaves to serfs. Governor Aiken owned one of the largest slave holdings in the South, the majority of which was employed at the Jehossee Island plantation. In town, a much smaller community of slaves inhabited the work yard, living in a series of small chambers over the kitchen and stables.

A PORTRAIT OF HARRIET LOWNDES AIKEN, PAINTED BY GEORGE WHITING FLAGG IN 1858, KEEPS
WATCH OVER THE DOUBLE DRAWING ROOM. THIS LARGE SUITE OF ROOMS, OUTLINED WITH ROBUST GREEK REVIVAL MOLDINGS AND
ILLUMINATED BY CRYSTAL CHANDELIERS FROM FRANCE, WAS CREATED DURING THE 1833 REMODELING OF THE HOUSE.

Today visitors are free to walk through this warren of rooms or the gracious sweep of chambers in the big house, unencumbered by the barriers of velvet rope that tend to cordon off the past from the present in most house museums. As a result, they can more fully experience the stark contrasts between these living spaces and more clearly envision the lives of both the wealthy inhabitants and their servants.

Fortunately for all of us, the custodians of this house have followed the preservation philosophy of John Ruskin, invoked in the 1975 newsletter describing the house's acquisition. "Watch an old building with anxious care," wrote Ruskin. "Guard it as best you may, for every influence of dilapidation. Count its stones as you would jewels of a crown; set watches about it as if at the gates of a besieged city . . . and do this tenderly, and reverently, and continually, and many a generation will still be born and pass away beneath its shadow."[4]

1. Middleton Papers, South Carolina Historical Society, Charleston, South Carolina.
2. Mary Boykin Chesnut, *A Diary from Dixie* (Boston: Houghton Mifflin Company, 1949).
3. Charleston Museum Newsletter, Spring 1975.
4. John Ruskin, *The Seven Lamps of Architecture*, 1849.

A LATE-1940S CAR WAS DISCOVERED "PARKED NOSE-IN TO THE GOTHIC ARCHED STALLS" WHEN CHARLESTON MUSEUM CURATOR J. KENNETH JONES UNLOCKED THE CARRIAGE HOUSE IN 1975. TODAY, A NINETEENTH-CENTURY CARRIAGE IS PARKED INSIDE THE BUILDING, WHICH HOUSED A HAYLOFT AND SLAVE QUARTERS ON THE SECOND FLOOR.

THE ONLY ROOM UNTOUCHED BY VANDALS DURING THE HOUSE'S DISUSE, THE
BALLROOM WAS CHARLESTON'S ANSWER TO KING TUTANKHAMEN'S TOMB. FRAMED BY THE BALLROOM'S HARP,
THE VANITY TABLE IN THE DRESSING ROOM BEYOND SUGGESTS A SUPERNATURAL VISITATION.

UNVANQUISHED BEAUTY

The Nathaniel Russell House
Historic Charleston Foundation

Arched like a swan's long neck, an undulating staircase forms the centerpiece of the Nathaniel Russell House. Winding its way through the central hall, this magnificent free-flying structure joins three tiers of rooms, each laid out in identical suites of rectangle, oval, and square. This staircase connects the public to the private rooms of the house and invites visitors today to travel from the present back into the past. Now a museum of Historic Charleston Foundation, complete with Charleston- and European-made furnishings within and appropriate plantings without, the house functions as a time machine, easily transporting guests back to the era of the Nathaniel Russell family, who lived here in the first half of the nineteenth century.

The house tour begins in the entrance hall, an austere rectangular chamber separated from the rest of the house by a pair of glazed doors with bent wood mullions that offer only a glimpse of the stair hall's inviting curves beyond. In previous times, most tradespeople and uninvited guests would have gotten no farther than this room. Today, however, anyone willing to pay the price of admission is invited to tour the Nathaniel Russell House, a home described in 1857 as "beyond all comparison, the finest establishment in Charleston."[1] After the ritual incantation of "don't touch" has been uttered by the tour guide, visitors are ushered into the inner sanctum.

Here lived the family of Nathaniel Russell, a Rhode Islander who made a fortune in Charleston's maritime economy and married Sarah Hopton, the spinster daughter of one of the city's wealthiest merchants. With their combined fortunes, the Russells built a grand three-story brick house inspired by the late-eighteenth-century English architect Robert Adam. With its elongated proportions and delicately rendered Greek and Roman decorative motifs, the house exemplifies the neoclassical style popularized by Adam. Most likely designed with the help of Irish architect Edward McGrath, the house is built of locally made brick and ornamented with imported white marble.

When the house was completed in 1808, Nathaniel Russell and his wife moved in with their marriageable daughters, Alicia, age nineteen, and Sarah, age seventeen, and approximately eighteen African-American slaves. Although Nathaniel probably spent much of his time at the wharves and warehouses along East Bay Street, his wife was much employed at home with the running of the household, planting of the gardens, and participation in the city's elaborate social rituals.

Along with her mother, Mrs. Russell was one of early Charleston's most accomplished amateur gardeners. Her garden was described by William Faux, an English visitor to Charleston in 1819, as a "wilderness of flowers, and bowers of myrtles, oranges and lemons, smothered with fruit and flowers." Much of the plant material came from a nursery maintained

THIS FORMAL DRAWING ROOM IS SET UP FOR A MUSICAL ENTERTAINMENT, WITH
A FORTEPIANO FROM THE LONDON FIRM OF LONGMAN AND BRODERIP, CIRCA 1790, AND
HARP BY ERARD OF PARIS, CIRCA 1803. PHOTOGRAPH BY WILLIAM STRUHS

AT THE NATHANIEL RUSSELL HOUSE, CONSIDERED TO BE ONE OF THE FINEST EXAMPLES
IN AMERICA OF FEDERAL-STYLE NEOCLASSICAL ARCHITECTURE, THIS CANTILEVERED STAIRWAY RISES THREE STORIES
WITHOUT VISIBLE MEANS OF SUPPORT. PHOTOGRAPH BY WILLIAM STRUHS

by Philip Noisette, a French professional gardener employed by the Russells. Today, flowering trees and plants originally grown in early-nineteenth-century Charleston bloom in profusion.

Mrs. Russell was no less expert in the social arts and made full use of the elaborately decorated drawing rooms on the house's second floor to entertain the city's planter, merchant, and political elite. A towering Romney portrait of a Charleston grande dame presides over the stairway where Mrs. Russell once might have stood to welcome her guests. The subject's patrician air reminds us that there once was a time when only the privileged few were invited to ascend the stairs to the Adamesque drawing rooms whose ornate walls still seem to resonate with echoes of nineteenth-century revelry.

The second-floor drawing room is a richly decorated oval with windows, doors, and mullioned mirror panels arranged to create a near perfect symmetry. Here ladies and gentlemen gathered for dancing and musical entertainment offered either by the accomplished daughters of Nathaniel Russell or musicians hired for the evening. In the daytime, soft light and gentle sea breezes bathe the room. In the evening, a chandelier and wall sconces would have held points of light refracting in the mirrored panels to create a glimmering constellation.

A contemporary of the Russell's describes the sort of party that would have graced this room: "the fiddle, fife and tambourine delighted the youthful crowd. . . . A variety of cake, & wine, & fruit, & jellies, & all the nice things that could be collected were handed about. . . . They danced and the Band played during the intervals of dancing. At eleven o-clock some delicious little oyster patties were brought up with other things of the same kind, after which the gentlemen were invited to partake of a supper of Beefsteaks, and cold Turkies, some of which was brought up to the ladies. We retired at eleven, but the party did not break up until two o-clock."[2]

More intimate, yet no less elegant, gatherings would have taken place in the rectangular withdrawing room, which spans the front of the house's second floor. Here, seven floor-to-ceiling windows open onto a series of wrought-iron balconies that overlook the street and garden. The social repast of tea would have been presented here—a meal so ritualized as to make one eighteenth-century visitor exclaim, "this place offers no resources for making close friends. One must be resigned to preparing endless as well as ruinously expensive toilettes in order to partake of their sumptuous teas or else stay absolutely alone."[3]

Although the house's grandeur attests to the mercantile pursuits of its builder, a trader of rice, indigo, cotton, tobacco, and slaves, its history tells of the female inhabitants' concern with more altruistic pursuits. In 1813, Mrs. Russell and her sister, Mrs. Gregorie, helped to found the Ladies Benevolent Society, an organization devoted to the health care of the urban poor that still meets in the Russell House. Mrs. Russell and her daughters also founded the Charleston Female Domestic Missionary Service to

ABOVE: ON THE FIRST FLOOR, AN INTIMATE PARLOR PROVIDED THE FAMILY A PLACE FOR QUIET MEALS AND STUDY. THIS MAY HAVE BEEN WHERE REVEREND TRAPIER WROTE HIS CATECHISM FOR THE RELIGIOUS INSTRUCTION OF SLAVES. RIGHT: THIS BRITISH BRACKET CLOCK WAS IMPORTED BY CHARLESTON WATCHMAKER WILLIAM LEE.

minister to the poor and to African-American slaves. This organization built St. Stephen's Chapel so that the area's poor would have a place in which to worship. Mrs. Russell's granddaughter, Sarah Dehon Trapier, married a minister who resigned from the respected rectorship of St. Michael's Church in 1847 to establish Calvary Church as a place of worship for slaves. It was probably in the Russell House that Reverend Trapier wrote the first Episcopal catechism published specifically for slaves in 1855.

Two years after the publication of this catechism, the growing family of Russell descendants sold the house to the equally illustrious Allston family, who transformed it into a Victorian showplace. Governor and Mrs. Robert Francis Withers Allston lived in the house only a few years before they were forced to evacuate during the Union bombardments of the Civil War. Following the reversals of fortune that ensued, Mrs. Allston and her daughters opened the house as a female academy in 1864. Six years later, the house that had once been the site of the aristocracy's benevolent works was sold to the Sisters of Charity of Our Lady of Mercy, a Catholic order that used the building as a mother house and convent school.

Perhaps it is because so much living has taken place within these walls that the ornate rooms of this museum seem so strangely intimate. Despite the velvet ropes that close them off and whispered exhortations of docent guardians, the rooms bear silent witness to the passions and pleasures that played themselves out within their warm embrace. At the center of it all, the cantilevered staircase that was ascended by generations of aristocrats, whispering schoolgirls, and cloistered nuns, and which withstood the assaults of shell fire, earthquake, and hurricane, still stands as a centuries-old reminder of the city's unvanquished charm and beauty.

1. Allston Papers, South Carolina Historical Society, Charleston, South Carolina.
2. Izard Papers, Library of Congress, Washington, D.C.
3. Letter from Josephine DuPont to Mme Talon, January 25, 1976, courtesy of Hagley Museum and Library, Wilmington, Delaware.

CURTAINS, WALLPAPER, AND BRIGHTLY PATTERNED CARPETS ONCE ENLIVENED THIS
WITHDRAWING ROOM. THE BLACK AND GOLD CHAIRS WERE MADE IN LONDON, CIRCA 1800.

COLLECTING AND PRESERVING THE PAST

*The Home of Randolph Martz
and Gene Waddell*

Neoclassical architect Randolph Martz uses the words "floating, palatial, gemlike" to describe the second-floor parlor in the Greek Revival tenement he shares with architectural historian Gene Waddell. "Sometimes I feel like I am on a ship, the Queen Mary, floating through all the debris around me," he adds. While Waddell may liken his sun-drenched attic office to a ship's helm, the ground-floor rooms have a subaqueous quality lent by the flickering green light that filters through the vines enshrouding the house. If the house is indeed a ship, it feels a bit like an anthropological voyager, jam-packed with artifacts upon its return journey from some exotic place.

Collections ranging from books (over ten thousand of them), electric fans, bronze and plaster busts, architectural fragments, and prints and maps by Piranesi, Robert Mills, and an unknown Japanese military engineer serve as an eccentric ballast. All of these possessions share space in a modest Greek Revival tenement built in 1851 to provide housing for Charleston's growing population of middle-class free blacks. Due to nineteenth-century city legislation restricting areas where freed slaves could live, the neighborhood known as Radcliffeborough, north of the major artery of Calhoun Street, became a neighborhood fulfilling the housing needs of Charleston's increasing black middle class.

"When I first came to Charleston, many Charlestonians lived like this," explains Martz, who is a native Pennsylvanian. "They didn't 'decorate'— putting something up just because it was pretty. They lived with their possessions, their mementos, souvenirs, and debris. It's not so much decorating as cataloging. Everything tells a story."

Waddell, a South Carolinian by birth, concurs: "Our house is representative of the way that Charleston used to be, only more so. Even though our house is a little cluttered now, it is full of things that we acquired because we liked them, not because somebody else thought they would look good together." Although Waddell describes their decor as "secondhand," perhaps the title of one of the many books he has written is a better moniker for their prevailing style: *Collecting, Preserving and Exhibiting: A Theory of Museums.*

When Martz and Waddell purchased the house and its dependency in 1979, their goal was "to remember the people who had lived in the house and to preserve traces of each era."[1] They felt it would be pretentious to dress up the house that Martz describes as a simple wooden box. Instead, they removed partitions that originally split the house down the middle in order to create the large living and working spaces that fit their present needs. The removal of these partitions revealed *Through the Looking Glass*–style twin elements on every floor, including matching doorways, staircases, and mantels.

On the first floor, duplicate screen doors open off a junglelike garden into a foyer crammed with

IN THE FOYER (ORIGINALLY THE SECOND OF THE DUPLEX'S MATCHING DINING ROOMS) A
COLLECTION OF ARCHITECTURAL FRAGMENTS INCLUDES A CERAMIC EGG-AND-DART CORNICE MOLDING FROM SAVANNAH.

43

architectural fragments, artwork, and books on one side, and, on the other, into a kitchen furnished with 1930s state-of-the-art appliances and a collection of canned goods selected for their exotically homely labels. Beyond these rooms stretches Martz's cavernous architectural office. Although five pairs of nine-over-nine sash windows pierce the walls, louvered shutters provide privacy and protection from the sun. Wraparound bookshelves packed with volumes on art and architecture, including an entire case devoted to the work of Michelangelo, absorb what light and sound do filter in from the street beyond.

A large drawing table dominates the room. It is surrounded by several busts and an acanthus-leaf roof ornament that seems to wait like a giant Venus flytrap for the old electric fans that hover around like oversized insects. These provide the house's only cooling system, augmented in summer by the shade of the creeping coral vine.

Martz's selection of this room for his architectural practice is an appropriate use of the space that once served as street-front shops. "This office works well for me as an architect," says Martz. "After clients walk through the garden and into the house the words, 'But we have to be practical' just can't come out of their mouths."

Surprisingly devoid of books, the second-floor parlor has a pair of Greek Revival mantels, five busts (Augustus Caesar, Milton, Molière, Cardinal Richelieu, and Voltaire), multiple fans, a pair of lyreback "gondola" chairs, and an Empire-style sofa with a rare cornucopia and lion's paw motif. It is here and in the garden that Martz and Waddell spend most of their leisure hours. Off this room is a large bathroom where a plaster bust of the Borghese Mars shares space with an Empire dressing table, a Gothic antebellum wardrobe, and a claw-foot tub. Another doorway off the parlor leads into Martz's bedroom, where the goddess Athena keeps an eye upon several cherished heirlooms, including a quilt fashioned by Martz's grandmother and wooden toys carved by his grandfather.

Above it all is the garret office and bedroom where Waddell spends endless hours of lucubration, turning out tomes on architectural matters both foreign (he recently completed a book regarding Canadian architect Arthur Erickson) and domestic (including a *Guidebook to South Carolina Architecture* from Oxford University Press and the Society of Architectural Historians). Here, high above the streets of Charleston, Waddell muses about the changes he has seen in the city over the decades he has studied it. "The biggest change I've seen in Charleston is how much more it looks like everywhere else," he laments, referring to the advent of bland contemporary architecture and chain stores downtown. "It is still a tremendous pleasure to walk around Charleston," he admits, describing a recent stroll to the grocery store that took him by three Greek Revival "temples."

To Waddell and Martz, true Charleston style is a concoction of beauty and decay that is too strong

PAGES 44–45: SECOND-FLOOR PARLORS ARE COMMON IN CHARLESTON, PROVIDING ACCESS TO COOLING BREEZES AND RELIEF FROM THE NOISE AND ODOR OF THE STREET BELOW. "ONE YEAR DURING THE SPOLETO FESTIVAL, SEVERAL PARTICIPATING VISUAL ARTISTS WERE ENJOYING COCKTAILS IN MY PARLOR," RECOUNTS RANDOLPH MARTZ. "ONE OF THEM EXCLAIMED, 'LOOK WHAT THEY'VE DONE TO THE CEILING! HOW CLEVER.' I LAUGHED AND TOLD THEM THAT THE EXPOSED LATHE WAS THE WORK OF HURRICANE HUGO."

46

for the taste of many newcomers. Martz describes his collection of night-blooming cereus plants as a perfect metaphor for the decline of true Charleston style. This gangly Amazonian cactus achieves perfect beauty once a year, spawning fragrant lilylike blooms that endure only at nighttime, preferably during the full moon. These plants were once quite popular in Charleston drawing rooms. Because they require summer heat to bloom, the modern prevalence of air conditioning has turned them into a threatened species. "The new breed of Charlestonians aren't patient enough to wait for the bloom," exclaims Martz. "They won't put up with something ugly for that long."

1. Elizabeth Hunter, "Preserving history, scars and all," *House Beautiful*, October 1992, 123.

THE ARTWORK IN THE BATHROOM INCLUDES A PLASTER BUST OF THE BORGHESE MARS, A CERAMIC TILE FRIEZE FROM SEVENTEENTH-CENTURY TURKEY, A CHINESE COMMUNIST POSTER, AND AN "OAXACAN NIGHT OF THE DEAD" BOX.

OLD-FASHIONED MODERNISM

A Radcliffeborough Dependency Apartment
Home of Leigh Magar and Johnny Tucker

Modern and old-fashioned, practical and romantic, minimalist and lushly textured at the same time, this nineteenth-century dependency is an architectural conundrum. The landscape gardener who lived here recently rooted much of the plant material in the overgrown garden without. The architect who followed made few changes in the house, which reminded her of Mies van der Rohe's Farnsworth House, with its single volume of space divided by a double-faced chimney. Johnny Tucker, current tenant and self-defined minimalist architect, admires the efficient, open plan and honest, unadorned materials: brick floor, unfinished tongue-and-groove siding, bare ceiling joists. "Everything is what it is," he explains.

What seems like pared-down modernism to these contemporary design professionals, however, is the age-old translation of "form follows function" that dictates simple, inexpensive solutions for efficient living. Like the house next door, also owned by Randolph Martz and Gene Waddell, this dependency was divided vertically in half to house two families; hence the pair of rooms on each floor with mirror-image staircases connecting one story to the next and a single chimney with four open fireplaces serving each room. Built originally in 1851 as a kitchen dependency to the larger house, this build-ing was subdivided into a residential duplex by 1861. By the turn of the century, one-story kitchen and bathroom wings were added to either side.

In spite of the house's essentially practical plan, Tucker's wife, Leigh Magar, recognizes its more poetic aspects. "You almost feel hidden here," she says of the cottage that is like a child's playhouse tucked away in the back of a garden. She confesses a lifelong fascination with tiny cottages and narrow corridors and a childhood penchant for playing with her grandmother's doll house. "I feel safe here, enclosed," she elaborates.

Original inhabitants of this simple, practical structure would have scoffed at these flights of fancy. By the time Randolph Martz purchased it in 1979, it had deteriorated so completely that it took Martz three years to transform it into a habitable building. The work included laying a brick floor, tearing down partitions, and partially enclosing two staircases with unfinished paneling that reveals the zigzag pattern of the stringers. The project belies both Martz's training in the International Style, which prevailed at Carnegie Mellon, where he studied architecture, and his familiarity with traditional, vernacular materials gained during an eight-year association with native Charlestonian restoration contractor Herbert DeCosta.

What is perhaps most striking about the house, however, is the sense it creates of being inside and outside simultaneously. Along the street side of the house, a series of tall windows and screened doors open onto the sidewalk. Masked by Venetian

SEVERAL GENERATIONS OF RESIDENTS HAVE ADDED INTERIOR WALL SURFACES SELECTED
FROM MATERIAL OFTEN CAST OFF BY THE REMODELING EFFORTS OF WEALTHIER CHARLESTONIANS.
VICTORIAN DOUBLE-BEADED PANELING COVERS THE DINING ROOM'S EXTERIOR WALLS.

inside and clinging coral vine outside, these openings emit a filtered light that dances on the brick floor and walls, which might as easily mark the parameters of a garden as an indoor space.

"I feel like I am outside when I am working in my studio," says Magar, whose millinery workshop fills one of the two first-story living rooms. Her fanciful hats sway like brightly colored blossoms from a series of hanging hat racks. The tiny room feels like an indoor garden that blooms inversely to the seasons: spring hats in fall and winter, winter hats in spring and summer.

Beyond Magar's studio lies the dining room, a shaded grotto where an austere table set for two is pulled up close to the hearth. An art nouveau chandelier and crumbling plaster the shade of pistachio ice cream invokes the decadent air of the bordellos that were sprinkled throughout this area until recent decades. The stairwell from this room leads to a bare-bones drawing room that Tucker uses as his

home studio. Although he has yet to install a computer here, he describes the room as "very modern" because the windows facing three exposures essentially transform it into a glass box. Certainly few modern amenities spoil the rough-hewn minimalism of the bedroom next door, which the couple heats with the wood-burning fireplace.

One of the most modern household appliances to be found in this home is a 1930s refrigerator that provides a distinctive silhouette in the kitchen. Through the kitchen door, the garden beckons with a blue glow at night emitted by strings of Christmas lights left up year round. Just as the rooms inside the house seem to dissolve into the outside space, so the garden spaces feel more distinctly like actual "rooms" than most. Directly behind the house, an outdoor sitting area is almost completely enclosed by the exterior wall of the house on one side, a screen of bamboo on another, and a collection of louvered shutters on the third.

PAGES 50–51: DAPPLED LIGHT PENETRATES THE SCREEN OF OLD SHUTTERS, PALMETTO FRONDS, AND DENSE BAMBOO
THAT ENCLOSES THIS GROTTO BEHIND THE DEPENDENCY. THE SHUTTERS WERE FOUND IN THE STREET AFTER HURRICANE HUGO TORE
THEM FROM NEIGHBORING HOUSES AND TOSSED THEM INTO THE GUTTER. ABOVE: TONGUE-AND-GROOVE PANELING IN HEART OF PINE
LINES THIS SIMPLE BEDROOM, WHERE A HAND-STITCHED QUILT PROVIDES COLORFUL RELIEF FROM AGE-DARKENED WOOD.

Between the dependency and the big house is an atrium-like space surrounded by the exterior walls of the two houses, metal fencing masked by dense banana plants, and curtains of climbing vines and roses. Here neoclassical forms of urn and obelisk hold court with an ever-changing array of derelict chairs, providing a sanctuary from the labors of all the inhabitants of these two houses.

"When I am working, I like to go out there beneath the canopy of banana leaves and catch a breath," says Magar. While she may view the garden as a peaceful sanctuary, Martz sees it as a more dynamic place. "A sort of Darwinian survival-of-the-fittest evolution rules my garden," says the architect, who has watched a variety of plants choke each other out of the small plot over the nearly twenty years he has lived there. Doves frequently seek its shaded privacy, as do mosquitoes, which Martz combats with an industrial size standing fan that keeps the air moving on sultry days.

The words of Whitney Powers, a local architect who once lived in the dependency, perhaps best sum up the eccentric, elusive charm of this establishment: "more like what I thought Charleston would be than what Charleston really is."[1]

1. Elizabeth Hunter, "Preserving History, Scars and All," *House Beautiful*, October 1992, 123.

A GREEK REVIVAL MANTEL, IDENTICAL TO THOSE FOUND IN MARTZ AND WADDELL'S HOUSE NEXT DOOR, WARMS THIS WORKROOM WHERE LEIGH MAGAR'S HAND-BLOCKED HATS AWAIT SHIPMENT TO BARNEYS AND THE HAT SHOP IN NEW YORK.

PENTIMENTO

Past and Present

PENTIMENTO

Past and Present

In art historical terms, pentimento refers to the translucent layering of past and present, a passage in a painting where the previous image shines through the final composition of oil and pigment. A misplaced limb, a hidden figure, or a lost landscape shimmers through the uppermost surface of paint, reminding us that beauty is more than skin deep. These images from the past that come dazzling through the present offer proof that time does not just travel in one direction, racing heedlessly toward the future, but also lingers and loops back upon itself.

Pentimentos abound in Charleston, where time seems to lag and even to stand still upon occasion. On many old walls, venerable bricks peek out beneath a newer veil of mortar, revealing the work of enslaved hands that built the city's structures. Underfoot in garden paths, old pavings trip up strolling feet in sharp reminders that the past is only hiding momentarily beneath thin layers of soil. Half-stripped surfaces in aging homes reveal the fanciful brushwork of long dead artisans: *faux marbre* mantels, gilded moldings, and architectural imaginings akin to those of artists in Pompeii. Ghosts are said to frequent certain rooms and gardens.

Old habits die as hard as lingering souls in Charleston. The St. Cecilia's Ball still takes place within the historic Hibernian Hall, whose gilded chandeliers have shone down upon generations of waltzing Charlestonians. At the Huguenot Church, worshipers still whisper prayers in French each year. In autumn, foxhunts and steeplechase events still clamor through Low Country fields. Fishermen cast nets into the shallow waterways to gather sweet creek shrimp, and oyster hunters dredge up muddy clusters of the briny mollusks that nourished Native Americans long before the Europeans landed.

Aural pentimentos haunt the place as well. The clip-clop of horse's hooves compete with the revving of motor cars. Measured chimes and tumbling peals of bells—some as old as the city herself—hang in the air. Street vendors no longer call their wares in the sing-song voices made famous in Gershwin's *Porgy and Bess*, but the basket weavers who sit on the sidewalks still hum hymns and Gullah tunes. Mockingbirds call out the same patchwork of songs they have since before the city's first brick was laid, although there are those people who insist that they also mock the tones of car alarms and telephones.

The city's many house museums offer visitors the opportunity to peek through the present into the past and imagine ways of being in centuries long gone. Simply by stepping off the street into these homes, visitors pull back the sheer veil that separates the present from the past. While some of these museums cast their spell by leaving things alone—torn strips of wallpaper and faded hints of richly painted walls—in others, carefully researched interpretations magically erase the trace of time. Refurbished rooms with bright fresh paint and gleaming furniture seem to await the

IN THIS ENTRANCE HALL, GREEK REVIVAL MOLDINGS, LATE-NINETEENTH-CENTURY ENCAUSTIC TILE, GILDED BRONZE LIGHT FIXTURES, AND TWO PAINTINGS BY CONTEMPORARY CHARLESTON ARTIST KAT HASTIE REFLECT 150 YEARS OF DECORATIVE DETAILING.

return of families long buried beneath the earth.

Many private homes perform the same sleights of hand. Walls left bare reveal the aging beauty of original decorative paint and crumbling plaster. Drawing rooms and dining rooms are arranged the way they have been for generations. Cherished antiques are treated more like old family friends than museum specimens.

Other homes play different kinds of tricks with time. The past and the present coexist in startling counterpoint. Old architecture and new stands side by side. Contemporary art adorns a wall outlined with Greek Revival cornices. Eclectic furnishings traversing centuries play variations upon themes of shape, color, and style. With what seems like shocking insouciance, Charlestonians jumble up the past and present to create anachronistic rooms and gardens.

These juxtapositions, rather than undermining Charleston's historic style, pay tribute to it. Charlestonians were never a hopelessly retrograde people. Only the best and most au courant was acceptable to its wealthy citizens, as evidenced by the frequent remodelings that changed the faces of the city's buildings. Many a Georgian or Federal facade received "modern" embellishments in Greek Revival, Second Empire, and Victorian styles. More than once, old-fashioned paintings and furnishings were moved aside to accommodate modish accoutrements. After the Civil War, families forced to live within limited means learned how to creatively mix and match the treasures that survived invasion and postwar economic devastation.

While there are those who would rather capture Charleston's grace in the amber of nostalgia, others revel in a millennial eclecticism. Hints of decay that celebrate the passage of time are left untouched. The antique and the modern playfully interact. New gardens bloom with vintage plants and old ones receive modern transplants like welcome guests. This is the substance of Charleston's pentimentos, shimmering layers of time's residue that succeed neither in stopping the clock nor in speeding it up, but simply render time irrelevant for a moment or two.

A MIX OF ANTIQUITIES FROM EGYPT, SYRIA, AND CHINA
AND CONTEMPORARY ART SHARE THE LIVING ROOM OF THE JOSEPH LEGARE HOUSE.

SOUTH BATTERY PENTIMENTO

The Stevens-Lathers Mansion
Home of Kat and Drayton Hastie

The history of this South Battery mansion is as colorful as the encaustic mosaic that decorates its grand entrance hall. Over the last 150 years, its owners have included antebellum cotton factors, an anti-Secessionist entrepreneur, and a Reconstruction-era financier. Guests at the house and its adjacent inn have included Confederate soldiers, southern socialites, northern notables (including William Cullen Bryant), floozies, ladies, and many others. Legends include the ghost of a Confederate soldier who haunts the rooms at the inn behind the house and the near death of the present owner's grandmother who, as a child, plunged through the ballroom skylight and clung to a chandelier until rescued by servants.

The building itself is a robust expression of the Greek Revival and Second Empire styles. Standing five stories tall, including the raised basement and mansard roof, the house is a gracefully imposing structure, clad in mellowed pink stucco and white piazzas. Set back only slightly from the street behind a wrought-iron gate and boxwood topiary, the building is one of the most grand and gracious edifices on the South Battery, favored neighborhood of Charleston's nineteenth-century merchant and planter elite. While the outside of this building, a modified single house facing the sea, is most distinctively Charleston, the interior seems to dwell in an international time warp that could exist in Venice, Paris, or even Pompeii.

Upon entering through the house's heavy double doors, visitors are enveloped in a three-dimensional chiaroscuro that defines the interior spaces, where shadowy rooms and blindingly bright chambers unexpectedly open into one another. On the floor is an intensely colored geometric mosaic of encaustic tiles that occasionally wobble underfoot. On the walls, the ghostly pentimento of architectural wall paintings stir memories not only of Charleston's past grandeur, but also of Pompeii's. A pair of gilded candelabra from Venice invokes yet another fragile seaside civilization. And down the hall, a winding staircase beckons visitors to journey deeper into the house's chambered nautilus.

Opening off this grand hall is a spacious double parlor that best expresses the building's original Greek Revival elegance. Deep plaster cornices and pilasters decorated with anthemia date from the house's original construction in 1843 for cotton factor Samuel N. Stevens. Running nearly the full length of the piazza, this room offers views of the Charleston harbor through a row of French windows. Divided by a grand piano placed at its center, today the double parlor accommodates both formal dining room and drawing room.

While some of the original Greek Revival elements survive in the hallway, the entrance and stair hall is a clear expression of the flamboyant Second Empire style imposed upon the house by its third owner, Colonel Richard Lathers, in 1870. Following Charleston's crushing defeat in the Civil War, this

BUILT IN 1843 IN THE GREEK REVIVAL STYLE, THIS HOME WAS SUBSTANTIALLY
REMODELED IN 1870 WITH THE ADDITION OF A SLATE MANSARD ROOF AND BRACKETED CORNICE. IN THIS
CENTURY, THE OUTBUILDINGS HAVE BEEN CONVERTED INTO THE BATTERY CARRIAGE HOUSE INN.

ON THE STAIR HALL WALL, KAT HASTIE PAINTED AN ITALIANATE MURAL CONJURING
PAGAN DEITIES OF SEA AND WIND COMMEMORATING HURRICANE HUGO.

KAT HASTIE FOUND THIS OLD MIRROR IN A ROOM BENEATH THE MANSARD ROOF AND MOVED
IT TO THE MASTER BATHROOM. THE CLAW-FOOTED BATHTUB CAME WITH THE HOUSE, AND THE
TERRA-COTTA HERB POT WAS PURCHASED AT THE DE'MEDICI PHARMACY IN FLORENCE.

native South Carolinian millionaire, who defended the Union in the war, purchased the house and hired notable Charleston architect John H. Devereux to carry out a ten-thousand-dollar renovation. The renovation included the addition of a mansard roof to enclose a fourth-story library "well stocked with books and engravings, and commanding from two sides noble views of the city and harbor," according to an account by New York visitor Alfred L. Dennis in 1874.[1] The project also called for the installation of pressed-tin ceilings, a floor mosaic, and the addition of a large ballroom, where Lathers held lavish receptions.

Lathers's intent was to use his wealth and Northern connections to help rebuild Charleston and ease her reentry into the Union with social and political gatherings uniting leaders of the North and South. Despite the elegance of these gatherings, little could be done to reconcile Charleston's elite to the renewed Union. In frustration, Lathers sold the mansion to Andrew Simons in 1874 and returned to New York. Simons, a defender of the Confederacy whose fortune survived the war, founded the First National Bank of South Carolina in Reconstruction times. He is the great-great-grandfather of the house's current owner, Drayton Hastie.

By the time Drayton and his wife, artist Kat Hastie, acquired the house, it had sunken into disrepair, ransacked by Hurricane Hugo in 1989 and abandoned for several years. In addition to major repairs required from a leaking roof and falling plaster, the house's decorative elements were hidden beneath layers of camouflage, including electric blue wallpaper in the entrance hall and coats of white paint obscuring the gilding on mirrors dating from the Second Empire renovation. But Drayton Hastie's commitment to restoring the house where several generations of his family lived, and Kat's deep affinity for the building's classical inspiration, fueled perseverance.

While renovating and running the adjacent Battery Carriage House Inn, where some of the more lurid incidents in the house's rich history occurred (this is where call girls stripped in the 1920s and 1930s and where ghosts walk today), the Hasties began the process of "excavating" the house from the residue of years of neglect.

"I felt this process of uncovering things was a bit like discovering Pompeii," explains Kat, who had already begun exploring Pompeian themes in her painting. "Hurricane Hugo was a little like the eruption of the volcano," she continues. Inspired by this realization, the artist painted an Italianate mural, conjuring pagan deities of sea and wind, on the wall facing the original architectural mural.

In decorating the house, the Hasties developed a style that complements both the opulence of the Second Empire and the elegance of the Greek Revival design. Many of the furnishings were inherited from Drayton's grandmother Kiki McAdou, the daughter of William Gibbes McAdou, who was secretary of the treasury under President Wilson. Kiki operated a Park Avenue dress boutique in New York

in the 1930s and 1940s and traveled frequently to Paris, collecting French antiques along the way. Whether a pair of yellow damask armchairs in the parlor, a satin-draped dressing table and stool in the dressing room, or mismatched Regency chairs upholstered in lavender silk, the decorative details exude an air of faded glamour.

Kat Hastie describes their style as a serendipitous "whatever we were given" combined with "trompe l'oeil" provided by her own paintbrush, which has touched everything from dining-room chairs to damask upholstery. An occasional new acquisition, such as the pedestal dining table lacquered black with faux inlay by a local sign painter and the reverse-painted, glass-top table in the drawing room, help to tie the stylistically diverse pieces together. Low Country interior designer Amelia Handegan, well versed in the art of eclecticism, lent her expert eye to the project, proposing a gilded ceiling for the master bedroom and woven grass mats for the drawing-room floor.

The end result is a three-dimensional pentimento of Charleston's rich decorative past and present, and the European roots that informed it. In a house infused with golden light that reflects from the harbor just a few steps away, time seems to fold in upon itself. And yet, life goes on. Grandchildren ride bicycles in the ballroom, ghosts walk in the guest rooms, and live models pose in the artist's studio that overlooks both Charleston and her historic harbor.

1. Robert P. Stockton, "Well-Known Architect Remodeled Mansion," *The News and Courier*, September 14, 1981 (quotation derives from letter written by Alfred L. Dennis of New York describing his visit on March 5, 1874, to "the beautiful house of Colonel Lathers on the Battery").

BENEATH THE MANSARD ROOF THAT ONCE ENCLOSED COLONEL LATHERS'S LIBRARY, KAT HASTIE HAS CREATED HER ARTIST'S STUDIO, ALTERNATELY PAINTING BY THE BRILLIANT LIGHT REFLECTED FROM THE HARBOR BEYOND AND SHUTTING IT OUT WITH SCREENS AND PANELS.

THE CHARLESTON WAY OF LIFE

The William Pinckney Shingler House,
Home of Dr. and Mrs. G. Fraser Wilson

Built during the last few years of peace and prosperity before the Civil War, survivor of siege, earthquake, and multiple hurricanes, the William Pinckney Shingler House and its contents offer testimony to the tenacity of the Charleston way of life. The handsome Greek Revival house was erected in 1854 for the successful cotton factor William Pinckney Shingler, who was soon after to sign the Ordinance of Secession and become a colonel in the Confederate calvary. Here, he and his first wife, Harriet English, held lavish entertainments in the spacious double parlors that could be used separately or en suite for large gatherings. Decorated with elaborate cornice moldings—a ten-inch-deep layering of egg-and-dart, acanthus leaf, and Victorian lace patterns—the rooms are among the city's most gracious. Matching carved marble fireplaces on one side provide heat in the winter months, while tall French doors opening onto the wide piazza and garden offer cooling breezes during the warmer months.

Today, the house is owned by Dr. and Mrs. G. Fraser Wilson, both descendants of early families who made their fortunes in Charleston's eighteenth- and nineteenth-century agricultural economy. Their heirlooms reflect the refined tastes and lifestyles of early Charlestonians and the love and reverence with which their descendants protect and use them. In addition to maintaining their own household, both

Dr. and Mrs. Wilson volunteer time to Historic Charleston Foundation and the Nathaniel Russell House. The Historic Charleston Foundation has copied several of the Wilsons' possessions for their line of reproduction furnishings, and the Nathaniel Russell House displays a number of their heirlooms.

Despite the beauty of his possessions, Dr. Wilson defines Charleston style as something less about things and more about a way of life. "The main thing about Charlestonians," he explains, "is their interest in one another, the way they love to hunt, fish, sail, and entertain." Dr. Wilson continues to describe Charleston style, using the house he has inhabited for forty years as an example. "During the Depression, the outside of the houses looked run down, but the interiors were nicely maintained. There wasn't enough money to buy new things, so the objects that people did hold onto were very well maintained."

Dr. Wilson describes a formality that ruled the households, a consequence of "so many people of different ages living in the houses at once." He also refers to a certain air of privacy that pervaded the home, using his elderly aunts who once lived on the third floor as an example. They preferred to spend their daytime hours in the second-floor parlor and come downstairs only for meals and occasional walks. "Grandeur we do not aspire, but privacy we demand," was their motto. Fortunately for them, they enjoyed both during their sojourn at the Wilson household.

Although the aunts are now gone, a host of elders remains to watch over things in the form of

THIS FRENCH PIANO, WHICH IS AN OCTAVE SHORT OF A STANDARD PIANO'S RANGE AND HAS BRASS HANDLES
ON THE SIDES, WAS PROBABLY DESIGNED FOR USE ON LONG SEA VOYAGES. IT IS MENTIONED IN THE PUBLISHED MEMOIRS
OF MRS. WILSON'S ANCESTRESS ELIZABETH ALLSTON PRINGLE, UNDER THE PEN NAME PATIENCE PENNINGTON.

family portraits, including a painting of Dr. Wilson's ancestress Mrs. John Porter by Samuel F. B. Morse and a fine rendering of Adele Petigru Allston, Mrs. Wilson's great-grandmother, by Thomas Sully. Throughout the house, these elders oversee an arrangement of cherished furnishings and bibelots that is richly textured without ever feeling cluttered. While many old, well-appointed homes have the chilly touch of a well-ornamented tomb, these rooms feel warm and alive, as if the varied possessions themselves had gathered for a joyous entertainment.

The house's furnishings weave together the many strands that make Charleston such a distinctive American city. Early English and European antiques, such as an eighteenth-century case clock by Joshua Lockwood, a French pillar clock, and Meissen figurines, reflect the penchant of early Charlestonians for importing European craftsmanship. The dining room's display of early Cantonware—brought back as ballast in clipper ships returning from China—is a reminder of the city's international importance as a major shipping port.

Charleston's prominence in the world trade led to a popularity of chinoiserie throughout the centuries. Evidence of this influence can be found in the upstairs parlor, where Dr. Wilson displays his collection of Asian artifacts, including a silk kakemono wall hanging and standing Buddha purchased during his service on the Pacific front in World War II. The Buddha stands atop an unusual piano made one octave short, most likely to fit within a ship's cavern during long sea voyages. Once retired from marine service, this piano took up residence at Chicora Wood Plantation in the possession of Elizabeth Allston Pringle. Flanking the Buddha are a pair of pagoda-form *tulipieres*, recent reproductions by Historic Charleston Foundation of the Chinese originals that were popular during the "tulip mania" that swept Europe and her colonies in the eighteenth and nineteenth centuries.

A private domain never included in the public tours that annually sweep through the ground-floor rooms, the upstairs parlor is home to a cache of objects that resonate with family history. The handsome Empire settee witnessed the engagement of Mrs. Wilson's parents. The books above it enriched the scholarship of Dr. Wilson's father, a professor of obstetrics and gynecology at the Medical University of South Carolina, as well as a teacher of French and Greek at the College of Charleston. The Hepplewhite chairs on either side were made in Beaufort by an African-American cabinetmaker shortly after the Civil War to replace the possessions lost during the destruction of the family plantation on Wadmalaw Island.

After the burning of Point Farm Plantation, one of the finest antebellum producers of sought-after sea island cotton, the Wilson family built a home in Rockville. It was here that Dr. Wilson spent many childhood years, surrounded by the possessions that he was later to inherit. "The dining room is my favorite in the house," Dr. Wilson admits, "because it looks so very much like our dining room at home."

PAGES 70–71: MOST OF THE FURNISHINGS IN THE FRONT PARLOR ARE AMERICAN, INCLUDING THE BANJO CLOCK AND THE HEPPLEWHITE CARD TABLE, WHICH WAS MADE BY A CHARLESTON CABINETMAKER IN THE EARLY NINETEENTH CENTURY. THE PORTRAIT IN THE BACK PARLOR IS BY THOMAS SULLY.

The clock and the portrait of James Hamilton Wilson by an unknown painter are both from that room, as are the floor-length blue curtains that soften the windows. "I would never have bought these draperies if I'd known there was going to be a market crash," was a common refrain of Dr. Wilson's aunt, who purchased them in 1929.

Like many of this house's furnishings, these draperies are sturdy survivors of both natural and man-made disasters. Although the mantel in the dining room is a replacement of the original that fell during the quake of 1886, most of the antiques have survived intact, outlasting even Hurricane Hugo. During the storm, which ripped the heavy shutters off within ten minutes and rocked the building until chandeliers and pictures swung from side to side, the house provided a sanctuary for neighbors and their pets. Built upon a heavy foundation of logs and bricks that was allowed to set for one year, this house was designed to last for centuries, providing a safe haven for the people who, with their possessions, carry on the Charleston way of life.

WHEN THE ORIGINAL WALLPAPER IN THIS ROOM WAS DESTROYED BY HURRICANE HUGO, IT WAS REPLACED WITH REPRODUCTION PAPER BASED ON A MID-NINETEENTH-CENTURY DESIGN FROM COLONIAL WILLIAMSBURG. ON THE MANTEL ARE CANDLESTICKS MADE BY JACOB PETIT, A FRENCH HUGUENOT LIVING IN ENGLAND IN THE NINETEENTH CENTURY.

THE SECRET GARDEN

The Joseph Legare House
Home of David Rawle

David Rawle's eyes light up when he asks, "Did you ever see the old movie *The Secret Garden*? It was all shot in black and white until you came into the garden, and then everything is in color. That's what I wanted my garden to be like." Rawle is talking about his garden, but he might as well be describing his house. From the outside, everything is monotone: gray stucco raised basement, gray clapboard, pale gray steps, gray door opening onto the piazza. But once inside, a kaleidoscope of unexpected shapes and colors unfolds. The first thing that meets your eye is a long glass table upon which regiments of toy soldiers display their arms. Above, a series of Andy Warhol's brightly colored Mao Tsetung portraits gaze benevolently from the wall.

There's little rhyme or reason to the collection of blue-chip modern art, time-worn antiquities, and hand-blown glass that fills the rooms, other than the owner's fancy. And yet, the eclectic collection seems right at home in the well-proportioned rooms, whose restrained Greek Revival detailing provides the perfect backdrop. "I think the integrity of the architecture here is so enduring that it invites you to complement it with whatever resonates most with you personally," explains Rawle, who admits that some old Charlestonians find his collection somewhat off-putting. "To me, this house says 'I'm secure, everything is okay, what would you like to dress me up as?'"

In the dining room, the answer was a garden. Childhood memories of his grandmother's dining room, replete with traditional hand-painted wallpaper of fanciful scenes, sparked a fantasy. "I had always dreamed of a dining room covered with work done for it specifically by one artist," says Rawle, who commissioned Billy Sullivan to create a series of pastel drawings depicting local scenes: Middleton Place, Bulls Island, Kiawah, Spoleto opera performances, and more. Attached to the walls with pushpins, these drawings create a new spin on the traditional hand-painted wallpaper favored by generations. Monet-like gardens, peaceful marshes, and a colorful picnic share the walls. Fantastical goblets and candlesticks of Venetian glass bloom like spring flowers on the shelves that line the room. Through the windows, azalea blossoms and a bright white dogwood tree echo their forms and colors.

Wall coverings of a different sort accent the living room across the hall. Here, Joseph Beuys's felt suit takes center stage, hanging on a wall between two windows where a more traditional Charlestonian might have hung a full-length portrait. "I think people who walk down the street and see that piece think, 'That poor guy hasn't had time to put his dry cleaning away,'" chuckles Rawle. Several more works by Beuys share the room with a nineteenth-century harp, two large sofas clad in lavender stripes, and a table full of ancient statues and fragments. "What I like about the antiquities is that they have an enduring serenity," says Rawle. "You feel like you are look-

A REPEATED PATTERN OF SQUARE, PINK-STIPPLED PAVINGS MAKES THIS SMALL SIDE
GARDEN SEEM LARGER THAN IT IS, AND MOVABLE CONTAINERS OFFER YEAR-ROUND VARIETY.

ing through time, both backwards and forwards." The same is true of this room, where the antique and the contemporary sit side by side enjoying a conversation of sorts.

Outside the house, the conversation continues as a turquoise table and chairs hold forth on the corner of the piazza. The unexpected tone lends informality to the white-columned corner that commands a view of eighteenth- and nineteenth-century rooftops covered with terra-cotta tile. Beyond the table lies a spiral staircase winding down into the walled garden below.

"I think I may own the only olive tree in Charleston," says Rawle, who planted it because he loved the way light looks upon its leaves. Here, as in the house, unexpected color and form play off one another to create a lively serenity. The paving stones, once gray, have been stippled with pink, which contrasts gaily with the bright green growth around their edges. Multiple containers of terra-cotta,

overflowing with magenta petunias and pale impatiens, scatter among the garden's marble columns and statuary. A bright, round orange captures a ray of light and holds it for a moment before the sun slips below the wall. Outside the walls, twilight shadows have already gathered into gloom, but within the secret garden one suspects that color will glow on into the night.

A STARTLING MIX OF ANTIQUITIES FROM EGYPT, SYRIA, AND CHINA, A NINETEENTH-CENTURY HARP, AND CONTEMPORARY ART SHARE THE LIVING ROOM. SEVERAL WORKS BY TWENTIETH-CENTURY GERMAN FLUXUS ARTIST JOSEPH BEUYS PROVIDE NOTES OF MODERNITY AND MYSTERY.

ART IMITATES LIFE IN THIS PANEL OF BILLY SULLIVAN'S DINING ROOM "MURAL"—A COLLECTION
OF PAINTED SCENES THAT LITERALLY PAPER THE WALLS OF THE DINING ROOM.

TRADEWINDS

Occident and Orient

TRADEWINDS

Occident and Orient

Enclosed by fortifications made of brick and palmetto logs, Charleston was one of the few walled cities in North America. While these thick walls protected inhabitants from understandably hostile Native Americans and even more dangerous Spanish colonialists, they were pierced along the water's edge by wharves that reached out toward the sea. These docks, called "bridges" in some early plans, connected Charleston to the world. By 1683, a Huguenot immigrant observed, "the port is never without ships and the country is becoming a great traffic center."

The ships that cleared the port brought in a steady flow of settlers from England, Ireland, Scotland, Germany, France, and the West Indies, seeking New World fortunes and, in many cases, fleeing religious persecution. They brought with them a host of traditions, including a range of religious practices, architectural styles, practical and ornamental crafts, and domestic customs. While these came directly from the West, they were interlaced with Eastern influence: barrels of Chinese export porcelain provided ballast, chests of Chinese tea and bolts of silk were among the high-priced cargoes, and several Asian plants took early root in Charleston's soil, including camellias, azaleas, and ginkgo trees.

By the time the last walled fortification came down in 1787, a rich array of foreign influence bore fruit in Charleston's rooms and gardens. Homes were built in architectural styles that reflected the prevailing tastes in Europe. Rooms were furnished with pieces brought over from England and France as well as those made by American artisans in European styles. Chippendale furniture in the Chinese and Gothic style enjoyed popularity, as well as Empire and Regency pieces bearing the influence of Egypt, Greece, and Rome. Tea grown in Charleston's own plantations or imported from the East was served in English cups, and English trifle was consumed from plates of Canton ware. While Camellia japonica trees bloomed without, painted facsimiles aloft with exotic birds graced colorful scrolls of wallpaper within.

Although Charleston enjoyed little direct trade with Asia in the seventeenth and eighteenth centuries, Europe provided the gateway through which various exotic goods and cultural influences traveled to the city. By the time direct American trade with China began in the late eighteenth century, Charlestonians had already acquired a strong taste for Asian imports. A mix of oriental and occidental treasures ended up for sale in the lavish shops of King Street, described in the 1850s by Charleston artist Charles Fraser as "so attractive, with its gorgeous windows and dazzling display of goods, emulating a Turkish bazaar."[1] To this day, boutiques and antique shops crowd the busy street with inventories ranging from English silver and furniture to antique Chinese porcelain and modish contemporary designs from around the world.

WHILE THE CHINESE-STYLE WALLPAPER AND FRETWORK CANOPIES WERE LATER ADDITIONS, MOST OF THE FURNITURE IN
THE THOMAS ROSE HOUSE BEDROOM DATES FROM THE EIGHTEENTH CENTURY, INCLUDING THE AMERICAN FOUR-POSTER BED, CARVED WITH
THE AMERICAN EAGLE AND TOBACCO LEAVES, AND THE ENGLISH CHINESE CHIPPENDALE GILT MIRROR OVER THE MANTEL.

ALTHOUGH THE COLOR OF THE STAIR HALL'S WALLS IN THE JONES-HOWELL HOUSE WAS INSPIRED BY INDIAN SANDSTONE,
THE FAUX-MASONRY DETAILING OF THIS NICHE, DISPLAYING DRIED GOURDS, IS IN KEEPING WITH WESTERN MOTIFS.

While traditional interiors in many of Charleston's homes demonstrate the distinctly westernized interpretation of Chinese form known as chinoiserie, more modern importations and interpretations of Asian style make clear that Eastern influence continues to evolve on Charleston soil. For example, a painted screen in the oriental style by Charleston Renaissance artist Anna Heyward Taylor depicts a Carolina parakeet. The screen hangs on a wall above a Hepplewhite sideboard, which bears an English silver tea service. The contemporary house in which this tableau stands is surrounded by modern interpretations of both Italian and Japanese gardens.

In another house, owned by the descendant of Charleston rice and cotton magnates, rice chests and textiles from Charleston, Burma, Sumatra, India, and China stand side by side in an eclectic mélange, reflecting the diversity of the city's current international trade while referring to the two agrarian staples of the mercantile economy in centuries past. The entrance hall is painted with faux masonry that emulates the golden sandstone blocks of Indian ruins. The bedroom resembles a British colonial retreat. In a mood of pure caprice, the owners commissioned a local artist to copy the walls of old Pompeii for a room that shelters shimmering Asian silks and exotic jewelry.

Charlestonians are like the Chinese, according to one popular and politically incorrect old saw, because they worship ancestors, eat rice, and speak a foreign tongue. Other more poetic similes compare this watery metropolis to Venice, "not because its thoroughfares are canals (although some do take on that appearance when a heavy rain coincides with a high tide)," explains historian Robert Stockton, but also because the venerable buildings lie "clustered on low-lying land which appears to float upon the waters of estuaries."[2]

Whole lanes look as if they have been transported, brick by brick, from Bath or London. Rooms might have traveled magically from ancient Rome or old Peking. Gardens could have been transplanted from the earth of France, or Italy, or Japan. Thanks both to its location in one of the great natural harbors of the world and to the lavish taste of its people for all things bright and beautiful, Charleston was, and continues to be, a gateway for a panoply of cultures that leaves its marks upon the city's walls and in its soil.

1. Charles Fraser, *Charleston Sketchbook, 1796–1806* (Charleston: Carolina Art Association, Gibbes Art Gallery, 1959) quoted in Poston, *The Buildings of Charleston*, 336.
2. Robert P. Stockton, *The Great Shock*, (Easley, S. C.: Southern Historical Press, 1986), 1.

OLD MADE NEW

*The Isaac Motte Dart House
Home of Betsy and Gene Johnson and
Wortham House Guest House*

While the experience of walking into a period room in a historic house museum is almost always tinctured by the vaguely voyeuristic impression that one is standing outside looking into history, the sensation of entering the sumptuous yet airy rooms of the Isaac Motte Dart House is completely different. Here, one has the sense of entering a house freshly designed and decorated when the Regency style of decor was all the rage. More than 150 years of history simply slip away. The experience continues uninterrupted as one walks through the gracious center hall and gazes through the back door upon a tidy parterre garden replete with blooming roses. A pristine Gothic Revival carriage house completes the scene, against a backdrop of venerable brick and masonry homes that falls away to the horizon line.

Yet this was not the scene that first met the eyes of the contemporary owners of this Charleston single house, who purchased it after fifteen years of near abandonment. "When I looked through the windows, my mouth fell open," says Betsy Johnson, who bought the house with her husband, Gene, in 1993. There was no plaster left on the walls and ceilings, save the elaborate cornice moldings, ceiling medallions, and composition mantels, which miraculously survived intact. "You could see right into the mortar and tendon of the walls," said Johnson, who later discovered that the original Roman numerals inscribed by the early-nineteenth-century craftsmen still marked the beams. "We had no idea how far the house could come!"

The couple first began their remarkable renovation in the carriage house, which had been used as a dormitory from the 1930s through the 1950s. "It was like a shed with a dirt floor," says Johnson. But beneath the dirt was linoleum, and underneath that, a hardwood floor. The entire structure was covered with vines and one whole wall was out. Within nine months, the building, with its giant arched entrance, pointed Gothic windows on the first floor, and quatrefoil fenestration on the second, was once more habitable.

Today, this carriage house, decorated with an informal mélange of English and American antiques, contemporary furniture, and Asian decorative objects, is operated by the couple as the Wortham House guest house. A large brick fireplace, added by the Johnsons, provides a focal point for the great room whose windows look out over the facsimile of an English country garden. Only the unmistakable silhouette of palmetto trees provides a reference point that locates the place in Charleston, South Carolina. Above, three cozy rooms accented with eclectic antiques complete the building's cottage charm.

Viewed from the large back garden, the gray clapboard single house on the front of the large lot has the unmistakable presence of the "big house." High on a raised basement and ornamented with a

ALTHOUGH THIS GOTHIC REVIVAL CARRIAGE HOUSE, REMODELED AS A GUEST HOUSE IN 1993, FEELS DISTINCTLY ENGLISH IN FORM, A PAIR OF SCARLET LACQUERED COROMANDEL SCREENS PROVIDE AN EXOTIC ASIAN NOTE.

Palladian window, the house is reminiscent of plantation design. On each of three floors, two massive rooms open off a center hall. Well above street level, the windows in the rooms invite bright light and fresh cross breezes. The ceilings soar high, and where they meet the walls, elaborate plaster cornices detailed with stylized floral and geometric motifs embrace the rooms.

A plaster conservator required a year of labor to restore these to their original detail, removing layers of encrusted dirt and paint and casting replacement panels where the moldings were destroyed. Equally laborious restoration was required by the composition work upon the mantels. While the dining room's classical mantel is decorated with a delicate garland motif complete with tiny flower buds, the drawing room mantel bears a foxhunting scene that recalls the English tastes and traditions that were transplanted by eighteenth- and nineteenth-century Charlestonians.

The rooms themselves are decorated with a collection of fine English antiques, nearly all dating from the early-nineteenth-century period of the house, some of them family heirlooms and others purchased by the Johnsons, who have avidly collected for many years. Throughout the rooms are fine oriental decorative pieces, including vases, plates, bowls, and silk paintings that reflect the Chippendale and Regency enthusiasms for chinioserie as well as the couple's own affinity for Asian objects. Many of the pieces were purchased during a Navy stint in Okinawa, during which the Johnsons traveled frequently to Korea, Hong Kong, and the Japanese mainland to collect. Booty from their travels includes Imari plates, Ming vases, and the brightly lacquered screen that provides a scarlet highlight in the carriage house's great room.

Both Johnsons descend from families that have lived in Charleston and the Low Country for generations, and their heirlooms hail from city homes and outlying plantations that belonged to these ancestors over the centuries. The tastes of these ancestors, along with their possessions, have clearly passed directly down to these contemporary Charlestonians. Although the Johnsons have been married for more than thirty years and have two teenage children, the rooms they have designed look newly minted, a freshly decorated haven for nineteenth-century newlyweds, perhaps. With crisply pleated curtains and space upon the walls for portraits of subsequent generations, the rooms seem not to hearken back to history, but rather to anticipate the joyful lives of its present inhabitants.

IN THE DRAWING ROOM, TEA IS SET WITH A CIRCA 1770 ENGLISH TEAPOT, CUPS, AND SAUCERS UPON A GEORGE III TILT-TOP TABLE FLANKED BY DELICATE REGENCY CHAIRS. A PAIR OF NINETEENTH-CENTURY CHINESE VASES ADDS A BRIGHT NOTE OF CHINOISERIE TO THE MANTEL.

CHARLESTON FUSION

The Jones-Howell House
Home of Kit Bennett & Jan Levitan

The restrained Greek Revival facade of this house on Hasell Street offers visitors no hint of the exotic world that lies behind its brick walls. The approach through a heavy iron gate and up a set of marble stairs spanning the high-raised basement builds expectations for the traditional Charleston interior, with a mix of eighteenth- and nineteenth-century English furnishings, classically inspired decorative moldings, and a touch of chinoiserie. And while all of the above can be found within the house of Kit Bennett and Jan Levitan, their creation transcends tradition. Although most of the elements are, in one way or another, linked to the decorative past of Charleston, their free-ranging eclecticism, from wall paintings copied from Pompeian sources to a Ming dynasty camphorwood chest to a Carolina Low Country rice bed, forms a new fusion of Charleston style.

"We are going back to the roots of Charleston and forward at the same time," explains Jan Levitan of the style he and Kit have forged. "Charleston has always been a port city with access both to Europe and to the Far East. We collect objects from the East that might have been part of the import/export trade from Asia, such as porcelains, textiles, rice chests, and Chinese furniture, and use them in a traditional historic setting to make a contemporary statement."

Many of these possessions, particularly the rice chests and textiles, pay homage to the trades of Kit's South Carolinian ancestors, the Bennetts, who owned the Bennett Rice Mill, and the Swints, who operated the Graniteville cotton mills in the up country. Other pieces are legacies from these families, including Chippendale gilt mirrors, an Empire bronze chandelier, and mahogany dining-room chairs. But the single most prevalent influence in the house is a rambling Asian eclecticism that reflects the couple's wanderlust.

Kit and Jan met while studying archaic Chinese jade in New York. Since that time, they have traveled constantly, frequently visiting Indonesia, Thailand, and India. As a jewelry designer, Kit gathers stones and inspiration from a range of Asian sources. As collectors, the couple started their own import company to justify their habit of acquisition. After a lengthy sojourn in New York City, they finally settled in Kit's native Charleston, largely because the climate and the physical setting reminded them of Southeast Asia.

"We are drawn to places that have this kind of light, where the buildings are designed with an openness to the outside like those in colonial India or Dutch Indonesia," explains Kit from the vantage point of the piazza. This long porch, supported by Doric columns and furnished with Thai and Indonesian teak, wraps around two sides of the house and is accessible from within through both a door and several floor-to-ceiling windows. "We chose this house because it is very suitable for the mixing of these influences, with its light, its open space, and its elegant but simple detail," adds Jan.

IT TOOK ARTISTS ROBERT SHELTON AND MARY SILSBY THREE MONTHS TO CREATE THIS FACSIMILE OF POMPEIAN WALL PAINTINGS USING HOUSE PAINT, ARTIST'S OILS, AND GLAZES. THE PAPER INDIAN DEITY PINNED TO THE CENTER OF THE PANEL IS SWITCHED WITH OTHER FIGURES FROM TIME TO TIME, DEPENDING UPON THE WHIMS OF THE RESIDENTS.

Throughout the house, whether in small details or sweeping compositions, the East and the West mix in a gracious harmony. The long entrance hall, which parallels a pair of double drawing rooms, is painted to resemble the golden sandstone blocks of Indian temples. Yet the faux masonry of a niche at the top of the stairs invokes Western architectural forms. Fluted pilasters crowned with acanthus leaves frame the pocket doors that lead into a dining room decorated with Sumatran textiles, Thai Buddhas, and Chinese and English antiques. The walls are painted a deep shade of saffron inspired by the robes of Buddhist monks. The baseboards are marbleized to resemble the dining room's portoro marble mantel.

On the other side of the pocket doors lies the living room, also painted the shade of saffron threads. In this room, colorful umbrellas from Bali offer a whimsical touch. Beneath the gaze of the four faces cast in an 1820s bronze whale-oil chandelier, a host of exotic objects are arranged: vessels for holy water and pillows made of silk from Benares, Sumatran *tapis tua*—ceremonial sarongs woven with strands of gold—a Burmese Buddha, Ming reproduction chairs carved of Thai hardwood. Surprisingly, these high-impact objects all mix together easily. Kit suggests that this is because the Asian elements and warm tones exude a certain spiritual quality to create a place of serenity.

Perhaps the most exuberant conjunction of these influences can be found in the Pompeii Room. When the couple moved to Charleston from New York, Jan remembered his visits to the Metropolitan Museum of Art's collection of Pompeian wall paintings and hired Robert Shelton, a talented decorative painter from Charleston, to re-create them as a contrasting background for the objects from their Eastern voyages. Within this room's glowing walls lies an Empire sleigh bed barely visible beneath the layers of golden fabric that cover it. A quilt made of sari-borders veils the mattress; Indonesian *tapis tua* drape over the ends. Fragments from Thai Buddhas decorate the *faux marbre* mantel. A small table is laden with treasures including a Burmese jade cup, a Buccellati cigarette case inherited from Kit's mother, and jewelry designed by Kit herself. Between the windows, an Italian chest of drawers holds two large platters piled high with bracelets, beads, and Asian jewelry.

The master bedroom is more restrained, with a pale palette, massive furnishings, and generous draperies that evoke a British retreat in colonial India. The walls are lined with Indonesian rice chests. A Charleston rice bed takes center stage, draped with a Rajastani wedding textile. From the corner, a Tang dynasty guardian figure keeps watch over the treasures. Here and throughout the house, one is reminded that once upon a time, Charleston was just one more exotic jewel in England's colonial crown, providing rice, textiles, and even tea.

TEAK CHAIRS FROM THAILAND AND INDONESIA, AN INDONESIAN RICE CHEST, BALINESE WOODEN ANIMALS, AN INDIAN
TEXTILE TABLECLOTH, AND THAI HORSE PUPPET (ON THE FAR TABLE) ALL SEEM PERFECTLY AT HOME ON THIS GREEK REVIVAL PIAZZA.

EAST MEETS WEST

An Ansonborough Residence

Behind the discreet facade of this contemporary residence in Charleston's historic Ansonborough neighborhood, Eastern and Western influences conduct a delightful pas de deux both indoors and out. Upon entering through the gate, visitors find themselves within an astonishingly compressed Italian garden whose towering cypress trees grow higher than the width of the plot. The four green giants frame a narrow central axis to create an optical illusion of length that would have delighted Italian Renaissance garden tricksters. At the end of the axis, an abstract nude by a contemporary sculptor from Maine invites comparison to ancient statuary. Boxwood hedges trained in perfect semicircles flank the allée, behind which a wall of time-worn stucco completes the illusion of European antiquity.

A small gate in a corner of the garden leads visitors into another timeless place. Beneath a canopy of leafy trees, a perfect Japanese garden unfolds with gently undulating contours. A small arched bridge connects a path around the perimeter of the walled garden within which winds a frozen stream of stones. Designed in Kyoto, the garden contains elements of traditional Japanese gardens to create a microcosm of spirit and matter. Framed by indigenous trees, the garden combines both local and imported plant material and Japanese artifacts to create a lushly exotic retreat.

The house itself is designed to take full advantage of the garden setting. Large picture windows in ground-floor rooms and balconies above frame views of both the Italian and Japanese gardens. The furnishings within these rooms reflect the gardens' dual influences. A low Chinese table and silk cushions form a sitting area in front of the window opening onto the Japanese garden. An antique Chinese robe hangs above a simple English sideboard flanked with Chinese vases. A painted banner found by the resident's grandfather at the Imperial Palace in Beijing ornaments the opposite wall.

The large room's minimal geometry invites the placement of a series of seating arrangements laid out with eclectic flair. On either side of the oversized marble mantel stand two couches adorned by pillows covered with Indian mirrored textiles. Two antique Chinese parrots stand on the mantel beneath a large figurative painting by Boston artist Jennie Summerall, whose fields of bright color and pattern complement the Asian textiles in the room. Khilim rugs cover the floor, and a large Noguchi lamp glows organically from the corner of the room.

In the dining room, whose picture window frames the Italian garden's boxwood parterre, Eastern and Western influences continue to intertwine. The walls are rubbed with a shade of faded red accented with geometric patterns inspired by Indian design. Upon the large glass table in the center of the room stands a tiny Taj Mahal. Testament to Charleston's enduring fascination with the East, a screen painted

ATOP A TURKISH RUG, THIS LOW CHINESE TABLE PROVIDES THE PERFECT VANTAGE POINT FOR VIEWING THE JAPANESE GARDEN THROUGH THE PLATE GLASS WINDOWS OF THIS CONTEMPORARY HOUSE BUILT IN 1972.

by early-twentieth-century Charleston Renaissance artist Anna Heyward Taylor, depicting Carolina parakeets alight upon a branch of sasanqua, is reminiscent of Japanese ornamental screens. Beneath this, a simple Hepplewhite sideboard, possibly made in Charleston, bears an English silver service whose tiny flower ornaments repeat the painted sasanqua's blooms.

While the owner of the house confesses to a lifelong affinity for Asian things, beginning with a childhood fascination with a Chinese elephant figurine belonging to her uncle, many of the Eastern artifacts in the home were inherited from her family and her husband's. Objects that she collected herself cover a range of cultures, including Chinese, Japanese, Indian, Turkish, North African, and Portuguese. "The Turkish rugs did not suit the 1800s house we lived in for twenty-seven years," she remembers. "But here, I can do anything I like," she says of this house, where two gardens create an inter-

section of East and West within the heart of one of Charleston's most historic neighborhoods.

WHILE THIS CONTEMPORARY HOUSE LOOKS TYPICALLY CHARLESTON ON THE OUTSIDE, WITH A DISCREET STUCCO FACADE AND WALLED GARDEN, ITS INTERIOR IS MODERN AND MINIMALIST IN DESIGN, PROVIDING THE IDEAL SETTING FOR APPRECIATING THE GARDENS WITHOUT AND THE COLORFUL MIX OF EXOTIC TEXTILES AND DECORATIVE OBJECTS WITHIN.

THIS ASIAN-STYLE SCREEN DEPICTS PLANTS AND BIRDS INDIGENOUS TO
CHARLESTON AND WAS CREATED BY A LOCAL ARTIST IN THE EARLY TWENTIETH CENTURY.

ALCHEMY

Fantasy and Transformation

ALCHEMY

Fantasy and Transformation

Alchemy is the refiner's magic art of transforming base metal into gold. A scientific impossibility, it nonetheless captivated the imagination of many susceptible minds convinced that a certain set of circumstances might transform their fantasies of untold wealth and beauty into truth. Many of Charleston's earliest settlers were transported to the colony by visions of vast fortunes that could be made by plundering her rich soil. Many of them second sons, inheritors of dwindling estates, enterprising merchants, or skilled artisans, these colonists came to Charleston to fulfill fantasies of wealth and newfound aristocracy. The homes they built and furnished, the gardens they designed, the furnishings they ordered, and the lifestyle that they forged provide enduring testimony to the power of their dreams.

Although the city was vulnerable to strange fevers, Indian attacks, and ferocious tropical storms, its wealthy citizens found solace in familiar forms. Jacobean and Georgian houses sprung up along the bends of the Ashley and Cooper Rivers, and along the city's streets. Later, Adamesque and Greek Revival homes were built of foreign marble and slave-made brick. Formal gardens in the French and English manner flourished in the virgin soil, with foreign cultivars interwoven among lush, indigenous growth. Greek and Roman forms were borrowed for merchant temples like the Market Hall and Old Exchange. So many churches of various denominations and architectural styles were built that sailors viewing the steeples from the sea dubbed the town "The Holy City."

Slave labor was imported to support these fantasies. African Americans were taught to speak in English and dress in livery as butlers, ladies' maids, and carriage drivers. Others worked as landless serfs in southern fiefs to support their owner's dreams. Southern Secessionists fought hard not just to protect this bitter labor system but to preserve the entire fabric of their lives: the right to engage in the free and lucrative trade with Europe, which made their sumptuous modes and manners possible. With the loss of the Civil War came the collapse of their economy and an abrupt end to the fantasy it supported.

And yet, Charleston survived the war more miraculously intact than many other southern cities. "Beautiful as a dream, tinged with romance, consecrated by tradition, glorified by history, rising from the very bosom of the waves, like a fairy city created by the enchanter's wand," is how Charlestonian Arthur Mazyck described his home in the illustrated *Guide to Charleston* published in 1875. Written less than a decade after the devastating war, this passage makes clear that Charleston's charismatic grace survived defeat.

But much was lost. Without slavery, the planter aristocracy could no longer grow the labor-intensive crops that were the cornerstone of their wealth. Many families lost their wealth, their land, and even their homes in the Reconstruction era.

SEEN CLOSELY, THE GILDED DETAILS OF CHARLESTON'S DRAWING ROOMS HINT AT THE
FLIGHTS OF FANCY THAT INSPIRED THEIR ARTISANS AND INHABITANTS.

Plantations were abandoned to ravages of weather and decay. In town, houses were closed off room by room, and beautifully appointed exteriors began to crumble, rot, and shed their paint. Even though some fortunes were regained and new ones made, the proud city had surrendered much of its former glory by the time the century turned.

Charlestonians kept their former dreams alive by clinging to the talismanic objects that invoked the past. This passion fueled the most successful historic preservation movement in America. As outsiders swept down upon the city to purchase cheaply the spoils of war, the men and women of the town organized resistance. They also challenged their own citizens who, in the name of progress, threatened to tear down structures that carried in their beams the city's former dignity and pride. As a result, Charleston ultimately emerged the victor over both war and time.

Preservation was also carried on within the walls, as Charleston families gathered up the possessions they had saved and forged a new kind of style born of reduced means and increased ingenuity. A kind of alchemy was practiced within the home as opulent effects were fabricated with broken and borrowed things. Fabrics were mended, splintered furniture repaired, and old rugs rearranged to cover spots of damaged parquet. Wood and marble mantels performed a minuet of sorts as those damaged during the war and the earthquake of 1886 were replaced by others that had survived intact. Peeling gilt and tattered lace became badges of honor; the new and the

perfect are almost seen as gauche among the old families who carried on tradition in drawing rooms and side gardens.

Together, these buildings, rooms, and gardens pay tribute to the power of fantasy to ignite transformations of near-impossible magnitude. The wresting of one of early America's wealthiest cities out of the marshy wilderness, the grafting of Old World mores and manners upon a brash colonial society, the resurrection of dignity and elegance out of a smoking war-ruined place: these are the transformations that have challenged skepticism and kindled pride among the city's inhabitants. Even today, as new threats emerge in the form of shopping centers and parking garages, the people of Charleston cling to their fantasies of beauty, grace, and charm that are the true substance of this city's wealth.

EXTENSIVE OUTBUILDINGS STRETCH ALONG ONE SIDE OF THE LARGE GARDEN BEHIND THE
WILLIAM GIBBES HOUSE, INCLUDING THE ORIGINAL KITCHEN AND WASHHOUSE AND ANTEBELLUM STABLE AND
CARRIAGE HOUSE, NOW TRANSFORMED INTO A SMALL APARTMENT AND GUEST QUARTERS.

THE RESILIENCE OF FANTASY

Middleton Place
Middleton Place Foundation

Vita Sackville-West wrote in her 1933 poem entitled *Middleton Place, South Carolina,* "Stand I indeed in England? Do I dream?" Her husband, Harold Nicolson, concurred that the garden at Middleton Place was "as romantic in its way as Sissinghurst," the couple's own famous garden across the Atlantic. While these garden aesthetes measured the loveliness of Middleton Place by English picturesque standards of the late nineteenth and early twentieth centuries, the garden also passed muster under the rigorous guidelines of eighteenth-century French landscape design. During his visit in 1789, the quintessential Frenchman the Duke of Rochefoucault praised the "wide, beautiful canal pointing straight to the house," and proclaimed that "the garden is beautiful."

These words of praise, spanning a period of 150 years and a series of cultural divides both geographic and chronological, reveal the universal appeal of Middleton Place. These gardens, originally designed according to the style of formal seventeenth- and eighteenth-century French gardens and modified to reflect the romantic influence of nineteenth-century English garden design, marry the geometric with the natural. English roses, Japanese camellias, and indigenous oaks dripping with Spanish moss create a pleasing tapestry of color, texture, and scent. A walk along the garden's paths, sometimes straight and wide, often winding and deeply shadowed, offers visitors an easy hour or two of constant delight—whether at the sudden discovery of a secret garden flanked by marble statues or the unexpected vista of scalloped terraces falling away to reveal a pair of man-made lakes.

While it may be easy to accept the beauty of these gardens as a matter of course today, it is astounding to consider the fantasy and will of the eighteenth-century man who called them into being. Henry Middleton was born in 1717 to a family that was already established as part of South Carolina's genteel planter aristocracy. He was the grandson of Edward Middleton, one of the seventeenth-century English settlers who came to Charleston via Barbados, bringing with them a plantation lifestyle that included the slave code, a love of Old World elegance, and a frontier will to harness the New World's resources. Although Henry's father, Arthur, presided over the convention that overthrew the colonial Lords Proprietors in 1719, and Henry himself led the First Continental Congress in 1774, these Middletons eliminated the English aristocracy only in order to replace it with one of their own.

When Henry Middleton came into possession of the land that he named Middleton Place as part of a marriage settlement in 1741, he acquired what his great-great-great-grandson J. J. Pringle Smith described as "a pretty house site in a primeval forest on a bluff overlooking a bend of a river, and a vision." Clearly, this ancestor was seized by the desire to tame and transform this virgin landscape into one that

MOST OF THE GARDEN STATUARY AT MIDDLETON PLACE WAS DESTROYED DURING
THE AMERICAN REVOLUTION AND THE CIVIL WAR. THIS MARBLE FIGURE OF A WOOD NYMPH
TYING HER SANDAL, CIRCA 1810, IS ONE OF THE FEW EXTANT STATUES.

would rival and perhaps, by sheer audacity, surpass the greatest gardens of Europe.

The fulfillment of this vision took ten years and the labor of one hundred slaves working under the creative guidance of Henry Middleton and an English designer whose name and plans were lost when the Middleton library burned in the Civil War. The plan is rooted in the relationship of the site to the river, which served both ornamental and practical purposes to this property, which was not just a country retreat but also a rice plantation. Twelve miles up from Charleston, the Ashley River performs a ninety-degree turn. Before angling off, it forms a straight westward path that leads directly to the site of the Jacobean house that once stood there. It then swings to the north, past a series of low-lying rice fields, which form the garden's border on the river side.

The eighteenth-century designers of Middleton Place imitated and improved upon nature by creating a pair of perpendicular axes that parallel the river's bend. An east-west axis defined by terraces and plantings continues the river's straight approach to bisect the original house. A long rectilinear reflecting pool defines the second leg of the angle that parallels the river's changing course. The long hypotenuse creates the third axis, sweeping across a series of formal gardens, including an octagonal arrangement of parterres, a sundial garden with radiating beds planted with English and Chinese roses, and an English-style mount.

Laid out in a grid, these gardens vary in size and character. The two large parterre gardens offer gracious expanses of color and texture, with wide views over the river, the rice fields, and the mammoth moss-draped oaks that fringe their shores. Paths leading out of the gardens guide visitors into shaded walks where smaller enclosures planted with lawns, floral borders, and hedges provide intimate outdoor rooms. Although these once were not so densely grown, clearly the gardens were created to provide relief from the heat and occasionally oppressive Low Country sky. Long allées lined with camellias—the very first to be planted in the country—provide shady, petal-strewn paths that lead to the long canal, where swans drift upon the dark, reflective water.

Grand and lovely as they are, these gardens cannot prepare the visitor for the experience of discovering the terraced lawns and lakes that descend from the house site to the river's edge. Visitors today approach the garden from the land side, following a drive that circumnavigates a park of grass cropped short by sheep. Although a hipped-roof flanker remains intact off to the side, a small pile of brick and masonry rubble is all that remains of the grand house that once ruled this estate. From this point, a lawn flanked with crape myrtles stretches toward the river and apparently drops away to the horizon. But a stroll along the well-groomed paths reveals instead a series of scalloped terraces that slope down to the river bank, where the earth and water rearrange themselves into the shape of butterfly wings.

PAGES 106–107: NEARLY 85 FEET TALL, WITH LIMBS SPREADING 145 FEET WIDE, THE MIDDLETON OAK, SEEN HERE FROM THE SUNDIAL GARDEN, MARKED AN INDIAN TRAIL IN THE DAYS BEFORE ENGLISHMEN SETTLED THE LOW COUNTRY. LEFT: RICE, A STAPLE OF THE LOW COUNTRY AGRARIAN ECONOMY, WAS GROWN IN THESE NOW FLOODED FIELDS. A SYSTEM OF DIKES AND FLOODGATES ONCE CONTROLLED THE IRRIGATION OF FIELDS BORDERING THE TIDAL RIVER.

While Henry Middleton's fantasy gave birth to this extraordinary marriage of geometric and natural form, the introduction of much of the garden's plant material can be attributed to his grandson, a second Henry Middleton (1770–1846). This Henry continued the plantings and expansion of the garden to feature many new cultivars introduced by his friend, the French botanist André Michaux, who brought the Camellia japonica, azalea, and ginkgo to America. Henry continued to refine the plantings of the French-style formal gardens and most likely introduced several of the elements that are more reminiscent of nineteenth-century English gardens, including the sweeping vistas and wide-open spaces dotted with giant trees.

Henry's son Williams (1809–1883) continued the legacy of landscape design when he extended the reach of the garden to include a vast azalea planting along the steep banks of the Rice Mill Pond, which reflects the springtime glory of the planting each year. But the most dramatic changes in the gardens of Middleton Place were wrought not by men but by the years of neglect that followed in the wake of the Civil War, during which buildings were burned, statues stolen or defaced, and the wealth of the Middletons destroyed for generations.

"Sad as a tomb crouched amid your tangled growth," is how Amy Lowell described the garden fifty years after the close of the war. "Step lightly down these terraces," she instructs visitors in her poem entitled "Middleton Place"; "they are records of a dream." Yet, the dream persevered under the guidance of new generations of Middletons who, nearly two hundred years after the garden's creation, undertook its rehabilitation.

"More or less a wilderness overgrown with tangled honeysuckle, southern smilax and bramble, yellow jessamine completely covering the great groups of camellia bushes," wrote Mrs. J. J. Pringle Smith of the garden she and her husband inherited in 1915. Twenty-five years later, they received the prestigious Bulkley Medal from the Garden Club of America with a citation honoring "two-hundred years of enduring beauty" as tribute to their garden restoration.

Under the supervision of present-day Middleton descendant Charles Duell and the foundation he created to perpetuate family stewardship, the garden continues to flourish to the delight of year-round visitors. Where once the power of one man's vision wrested from the wilderness a landscape rivaling the great pleasure gardens of kings, Middleton Place still blooms, a testimony to the resilience of this fantasy that has fueled generations of Middletons.

THE DIAGONAL AXIS OF THE GARDENS PASSES THROUGH THIS GEOMETRIC SUNDIAL GARDEN. WITHIN THE BOXWOOD
HEDGES GROW CHINA AND TEA ROSES, FIRST PROPAGATED IN THE EIGHTEENTH AND NINETEENTH CENTURIES.

STILL LIFE WITH HEIRLOOMS

The Home and Atelier
of Marty Whaley Adams

Anative Charlestonian whose family has lived in the city, on mainland plantations, and on nearby sea islands for generations, Marty Whaley Adams grew up surrounded and deeply influenced by Low Country lifestyles. But as an artist, she draws her inspiration from France and southern Europe, particularly from the still lifes of Manet, Matisse, Bonnard, and Vuillard. Certainly Charleston, with its worn grandeur, colorful palette, and sensual, tradition-laden ways is not too far removed from the world that turns up again and again in these artists' work.

In transforming the third floor of a severe classical revival office building from the 1890s into a home, Marty merged these influences to create a three-dimensional composition that is often depicted in her watercolor and monotype still lifes. The result is a bohemian suite of rooms filled with time-worn antiques, colorful paintings, and boldly textured handicrafts that might easily be mistaken for an atelier on the French Riviera, were it not for the decidedly regional flavor of the heirlooms.

While the rooms once had a distinctly masculine air as the library of the law firm presided over by Marty's father, today the male and the female, the pragmatic and fantastical, seem to coexist side by side. Some of the artist's innovations seem downright audacious for a former sanctum of the law, such as

the epigram from Albert Einstein that she stenciled on the wall: "Imagination is more important than knowledge." Or the fact that her father's partner's desk now serves as the kitchen table, with drawers that once held legal briefs storing linen napkins. Yet, as a whole, the apartment seems to reweave the distinct strands of the artist's forebears into a richly textured cloth.

The apartment fills the entire third floor of the building, and is entered from an elevator door which neatly divides the space into the facsimile of a center-hall plan. Visitors are immediately greeted by a sideboard laden with silver that shines with a rich gloss and is often filled to overflowing with creamy roses. Well-polished silver is found throughout house. "I love to think about the many generations of hands that have used these silver pieces and polished them over the years," says Marty. To set off the gleam of silver and wood, she painted the wall a deep blend of brown and black, a traditional Charleston color called *tête de negre*.

But if these traditional elements lull visitors into expecting the expected, they will be surprised when they enter the suite that forms the apartment's focal point. Exhibiting Charlestonian ingenuity in transforming utilitarian outbuildings into luxurious dwellings, Marty has created a sensual domain out of an utterly prosaic space. Where industrial carpet, floor-to-ceiling bookcases, acoustical tile ceiling, and dark wood paneling once formed the accoutrements of a legal library, a fanciful arrangement of the

THIS TABLEAU PAYS HOMAGE TO THE TRADITIONAL MALE PLEASURES OF PLANTATION LIFE,
WITH ITS BRONZE HUNTING DOGS, WALKING STICK, LEATHER BOUND VOLUMES, FORTIFIED WINES,
AND HEADS OF GAME. THE PORTRAIT WAS PAINTED AT BELVEDERE PLANTATION.

antique and the eccentric now exists. A *faux marbre* floor of painted Masonite covers the old carpet. The bookshelves have been rearranged to create room dividers and closet space. A weathered ceiling beam that was revealed when the hung ceiling was removed provides a rustic touch.

From the middle of the living room, a large four-poster bed is visible through a curtained doorway. Demurely veiled with ivory draperies, this bed has many tales to tell, including the time Marty's grandmother's cook hid beneath it to escape the wrath of her grandfather's buggy-boy. Or the time her grandfather chased her grandmother around the bedroom with a praying mantis he had plucked from its mosquito netting. This bed has witnessed the comings and goings of several generations, including the birth of the present owner's mother. Made on a nearby plantation, it has been enlarged and embellished with an iron canopy frame designed by Marty.

Reminders of plantation life are scattered throughout the home. To the right of the bed is an old sign promoting a horse race started by Marty's grandmother following the Civil War to raise morale and provide entertainment. Over a large sideboard in the living room is a portrait of Charles St. George Sinkler, the artist's great-grandfather and owner of Belvedere Plantation. Shown in the backdrop of the portrait, the plantation was one of the original king's grant properties of the South Carolina colony that passed through several generations of Marty's family before being flooded beneath the waters of Lake Marion in a WPA project. The horns hanging on either side of the portrait were collected by Sinkler's son-in-law, a country doctor who often received payment in the form of game, and once papered the plantation's hall with deer hides.

The bronze statues of hunting dogs came from Gippy Plantation, where the artist's Uncle Nick Roosevelt (second cousin to Franklin) and Aunt Emily lived. At the foot of the room is another souvenir from Gippy, a dining table of rich walnut and burled inlay where the Roosevelts entertained their family and friends, including cousin Eleanor. Above it is an early nineteenth-century painted Italian mirror from Belvedere Plantation and Marty's library of art and design books. During the daytime, the window to the left provides a view of the polychrome dome of the Gibbes Museum of Art. In the evening, the table is often set with old family china and lit by heirloom candelabra. The artist often photographs her table settings to serve as inspiration for future paintings.

Against another wall of the room stands a Chippendale secretary with yet another story to tell. This piece belonged to a distant cousin whose husband purchased it in Virginia around the turn of the century. According to the story, when he got home and found out how fine it was, he exclaimed, "I have not paid enough for this," and returned to Virginia to find the seller and offer him additional payment. Through the windows is yet another spectacular view of Charleston, including the steeple of St. Philip's

Church, beneath which Marty's parents are buried.

Marty believes that her father would approve of the changes she has made in his former law office, where she now maintains a gallery on the first floor and a studio on the second. "I've had to do a lot of independent thinking to do what I have done here," she says. "I've wiped out any thought of social expectations," adds this Charlestonian whose extended family helped to establish Low Country custom over the centuries. Perhaps it is Marty's very ease with local style and custom that fuels her cheerful irreverence for it.

Certainly, it is this ability to forge startling bonds between the antique and the contemporary, the traditional and the unexpected that makes Marty's home so like the satisfying composition of a still-life painting. Here, the sunlight gleams on the polished wood and silver, casting shadows upon the possessions of many generations. Although the clock by the window, another legacy from Gippy Plant-

ation, stopped ticking years ago, the church bells from the steeples without still mark the passing of time in hollow peals. As in every good still life, time stands still here just long enough to capture the complex juxtapositions of life and art.

THIS ITALIAN MIRROR HUNG AT BELVEDERE PLANTATION FOR MORE THAN A HUNDRED YEARS
BEFORE IT WAS RELEGATED TO A DUSTY CORNER WHERE MARTY ADAMS REDISCOVERED IT. ELEANOR
ROOSEVELT ONCE DINED AT THIS INLAID WALNUT TABLE AT GIPPY PLANTATION.

CHARLESTON FANTASIA

The Thomas Hamlin House
Home of Amelia and Jack Handegan

Charleston designer Amelia Handegan grew up on a plantation about an hour northwest of Charleston, on land granted to her family in the eighteenth century. Her early years instilled in her a deep sense of place: a love of time-worn architecture and furnishings; a taste for colors found in country fields, such as earth brown and chartreuse first-growth; and an understanding of how to make a house a home. Long country afternoons also gave her plenty of time to hone a sense of fantasy. These are the sources upon which the designer draws to inspire elegant interiors that are simultaneously refined and relaxed, formal and fantastical, like her own home in Charleston.

Handegan's flights of fancy soar high in the late-1820s house she shares with her husband and two sons in Harleston Village, a suburb founded by the city's entrepreneurs and intellectuals in the eighteenth century. Located on the western edges of the Charleston peninsula, the house once looked out over the Ashley River before landfill developments claimed the marshy banks. Accordingly, the design of the house is closer in form to the center hall plantations found in the countryside than to the downtown single houses. The rooms within, though not large, are well proportioned and elegantly detailed with restrained Greek Revival woodwork. Yet even before Handegan moved in, whimsy had begun to infiltrate the severe rooms in the form of four painted palmetto trees that rise in the corners of the dining room.

With her signature panache, Handegan took the ball and ran with it, installing in the center of the dining room a crystal chandelier with undulating palm fronds of bronze growing from its shaft. Continuing the juxtaposition of the formal with the playful, Handegan surrounded a table sheathed in gingham patterned silk with brocade chairs and arranged a still life of gazing balls and servant's bells upon the mantel. Modern lamps with steep cones of brushed metal shades flank an antique portrait of a boy above the sideboard.

Across the hall lies the drawing room, which is painted a deep shade of overripe pumpkin created with several layers of paint and glaze. In this, as in many of Handegan's rooms, she has taken the startlingly vivid palette of eighteenth- and nineteenth-century Charleston interiors—persimmons, strawberries, kiwi greens—and re-created them in muted tones, as if the pigments had faded and sunken gradually into the plaster walls. In a nod to the habits of old Charlestonians who replaced their silk and woolen rugs in summer with woven mats, Handegan unfurled a sea grass mat across the floor. Chairs and couches of wildly diverse vintage display striped, floral, and animal print upholstery. Portraits ranging from the formal to the primitive adorn the walls.

One can imagine with the same amount of ease great-aunts playing bridge within this room or the Mad Hatter offering tea to Alice in Wonderland. "I have always believed that a sense of humor is essen-

A WHIMSICAL ARRANGEMENT OF GAZING BALLS AND SERVANT BELLS ON THE MANTEL IS REFLECTED IN A MID-NINETEENTH-CENTURY ENGLISH MIRROR. THE CHANDELIER WAS MADE FROM A BRONZE SPRAY OF LEAVES FOUND IN AN ANTIQUE SHOP.

tial to design," says Handegan, who once went out to buy a plant and came home with an iron topiary stand instead, which forms an oddball obelisk in the corner of the room.

Two more rooms open off the house's wide center hall, a family sitting room with walls upholstered in brown and white ticking, and a bedroom of the kind that dreams are made of. Crystal tumblers filled with roses and camellia blooms adorn the bedroom mantel, above which hangs a mirror of flaking gilt and mercury whose murky depths seem less to reflect the room than to offer a glimpse into another century. A metal-leafed canvas by Charleston artist Kat Hastie nesting between mahogany bedposts on the opposing wall features a ghostly silhouette. A bedspread punctuated with chenille buds the size of popcorn covers the massive four-poster bed that dominates the room.

A fantasy of sorts plays out in the folding screen collaged with reproduction wallpaper that covers the bedroom's farthest wall. The screen depicts a pair of lovers clad in Empire-style finery who stroll through an impossible landscape featuring Venetian gondolas, Grecian temples, and a Roman campanile against a backdrop of Tuscan hills. Because translucent charmeuse draperies obscure the view outside the room's real windows, this screen takes on a surreal presence. Like a picture window, it seems to offer a view into the landscape beyond. For a moment, it seems possible that the canal flowing through its antique panels might be the Ashley River coursing toward the sea and back again in tidal

indecision beyond the house's walls.

This is the magic of Amelia Handegan at work—a skill for combining the antique and the eccentric to create a timeless atmosphere where anything is possible. Old lace and antique trims, paintings marred with craquelure, and mirrors with flaked backing merge with modern accents here and there to create what Handegan calls "perfect imperfection." It is this instinctive ease with a range of styles and forms, this lapsing into pleasing anachronisms, achieved by mixing fine antiques with found objects and the most au courant design that makes Handegan a quintessentially Charlestonian artisan.

1. Jonathan Poston, *The Buildings of Charleston* (Columbia: University of South Carolina Press, 1997), 479.

PAGES 118–119: THE DRAWING TABLE CENTERS AROUND A SMALL PEDESTAL TABLE WITH ROMAN FEET, MADE IN AMERICA, CIRCA 1830. ABOVE THE MANTEL ARE AN EIGHTEENTH-CENTURY FRENCH PORTRAIT OF A LADY AND AN EARLY-NINETEENTH-CENTURY PRIMITIVE AMERICAN PORTRAIT OF A CHILD.

A MID-NINETEENTH-CENTURY ENGLISH PORTRAIT HANGS ABOVE AN ENGLISH CHEST, CIRCA 1820.
CONTEMPORARY LAMPS OF LUCITE AND SILVER LEAF ADD A MODERN NOTE. THE CHANDELIER'S BRONZE FRONDS
PERFECTLY ECHO THE SILHOUETTE OF PALM TREES PAINTED IN THE ROOM'S CORNERS.

ARISTOCRATIC WHIMSY

Reeves Van Hettinga's
Dependency Apartment

One enters Reeves van Hettinga's world through a gateway carved with dueling dragons. The gravel drive passes the big house built in 1797, and enters a timeless place where tiny out-buildings of brick and slate lie caught in a tangle of vines and roses. Van Hettinga succumbed to the place's spell more than a decade ago, but had to wait years for a vacancy in the dependency apartments of this eighteenth-century compound. When the owner called to inform him of an available apartment, van Hettinga gave it about two days' thought before saying, "Yes. Yes!"

Within weeks, van Hettinga fled his apartment in New York City's West Village, "a tiny little studio with a Pullman kitchen and horrible neighbors," to take up residence in Charleston. Here, he found the perfect milieu to express his love of eighteenth- and nineteenth-century decorative arts. "In Charleston, you have a more florid expression of the eclectic influences that shaped nineteenth-century design than in Boston or Philadelphia," explains van Hettinga. "Down here, people had an aristocratic sense of playfulness!"

Certainly, van Hettinga succumbed completely to highborn whimsy in decorating the former laundry house and slave quarters he now inhabits. Well-versed in the art of alchemy (a French chef by profession who studied set design at the Yale Univer-

sity theater department in the 1950s), van Hettinga set about transforming the simple apartment into an imaginary treasure palace, using a few well-chosen antiques and a deftly handled paintbrush to create the illusion of many more opulent *objets*.

On the first floor, van Hettinga took inspiration from the arts of China and her Western cousin, European chinoiserie. A mural depicting a Chinese landscape dominates one wall of the tiny room. A Chinese Chippendale mirror is painted above the fireplace, which is, in turn, decorated with a *faux marbre* surround. On the walls hang Ming plates secured with pretty ribbons—all created by van Hettinga's paintbrush. A painted monkey displays a shocking irreverence for his expensive surroundings, poised with a priceless vase within its paws, ready to toss it at the slightest provocation.

Upstairs, the large bedroom expresses a free-ranging eclecticism not unlike the Empire and Greek Revival styles that influenced many of Charleston's finest dwelling places. The mural on the rear wall of the room summons ancient Rome, offering a view through a rustic stone arch of the Temple of Minerva Medica based on a drawing by Piranesi. Blue draperies in the mural take on three-dimensional form in the moiré bedclothes and table skirt created by Charleston designer John Ragsdale. Blue swags carved from painted plywood adorn the windows. "Rex Whistler did that in 1939 for an abbey he decorated for an English aristocrat," said van Hettinga of the wooden curtains.

THIS ROW OF BRICK DEPENDENCIES HOUSED SLAVE QUARTERS AND UTILITY AREAS, INCLUDING KITCHEN AND LAUNDRY, FOR THE LATE-EIGHTEENTH-CENTURY SINGLE HOUSE THAT STANDS ON THE FRONT OF THIS LARGE LOT.

AN ENAMELED PICTURE FRAME HOLDING A PHOTOGRAPH OF REEVES VAN HETTINGA'S MOTHER
ECHOES THE MALACHITE TONES OF THE PAINTED WOODEN FRAME ABOVE, WHICH WAS CREATED BY VAN HETTINGA.
THE MEISSEN MONKEY FIGURINE ONCE PLAYED A TRIANGLE, NOW BROKEN OFF, WITH ITS PAWS.

On the floor is a Turkish rug with lustrous tones that perfectly reflect the blue draperies and red walls of the room. "The paint was called Scarlett O'Hara," says van Hettinga in an aside. "A very fitting color." In the center of the room is a massive mahogany sleigh bed of French lineage and a velvet-clad armchair purchased from Pierre Deux. An elaborately painted mirror created by van Hettinga adorns one wall, reflecting the room's contents. "I wanted a slightly primitive Russian look with all that malachite," says van Hettinga of the mirror, "like something you might see in a Russian dacha in 1815."

On the opposite side of the room is a Biedermeier *schatzkabinett* (or treasure chest) of ebony and burled walnut. "I made it out of pine wood," van Hettinga confesses. Behind its fake glass doors lies an imaginary treasure trove of fifth-century-B.C. Greek artifacts including busts, vases, urns, and a golden armband. "Nothing but the best and most rare," boasts van Hettinga of the cabinet's painted contents.

"I am always creating my own fantasy," says van Hettinga of his designs. In New York, he created a neo-Gothic grotto, complete with moss-covered statues and vistas of an English garden in his studio apartment. In Charleston, he has conjured an old-world sanctuary replete with exotic artifacts "gathered" from around the world and throughout the ages. "Here I have created my own sense of place," says van Hettinga, who grew up in the suburbs of Chicago and Ann Arbor, Michigan. "This is as far away from Kansas as I can get."

"Without really thinking about Charleston, I have done something very Charlestonian," reflects van Hettinga about his new home. Certainly the selection of Greek and Chinese artifacts, with an occasional nod to *le style antique,* is in keeping with the exuberant eclecticism of Charleston's Empire and Greek Revival styles. But van Hettinga's use of economic means to create a grand effect is also a tribute to Charleston style: the sleight-of-hand practiced by Charlestonians who managed to maintain an air of grand dignity despite a decided lack of means in the post–Civil War days. This transplanted Charlestonian's painterly prestidigitation provides a whole new spin on the old saw, "Too poor to paint, too proud to whitewash."

PAGES 126–127: THIS SMALL ROOM IS TRANSFORMED INTO AN OPULENT BED-SITTING-ROOM, DOMINATED BY A MASSIVE FRENCH SLEIGH BED AND A COLORFUL MURAL DEPICTING THE TEMPLE OF MINERVA MEDICA, BASED ON A DRAWING BY PIRANESI.